The Ministry
of the
Child

The Ministry of the Child

Dennis C. Benson
& Stan J. Stewart

ABINGDON
NASHVILLE

THE MINISTRY OF THE CHILD

Copyright © 1978 and 1979 by Dennis C. Benson and Stan J. Stewart

Library of Congress Cataloging in Publication Data

BENSON, DENNIS C
    The ministry of the child.
    1. Children—Religious life. I. Stewart, Stanley J., 1937- joint
author. II. Title.
BV4571.2.B46   248'.82   78-12003

ISBN 0-687-27039-1

MANUFACTURED BY THE PARTHENON PRESS AT
NASHVILLE, TENNESSEE, UNITED STATES OF AMERICA

FOREWORD

Dennis Benson and Stan Stewart have with this book created a gift for adults who want to keep on growing. It's obvious that these men have not closed the doors between their own childhood experiences and their present. They themselves can help lead us—through these sensitive stories of ministering children—to our own Starchild within, because they are obviously so much in touch with their own.

How do children minister in hospitals, in church services, in polio wards, in airplanes, in grief, in joy? Stan and Dennis have observed and participated in the healing of children with such compassion it pleases me to think of the many young lives these men—on two different continents—have touched.

Before this book was written its growing message in the hearts of the authors was a gift to the children they knew. Now it's a gift to the child in all of us—the Starchildren. I, for one, thank them for their love and their work.

Fred Rogers
"Mister Rogers' Neighborhood"

CONTENTS

THE AUTHORS SPEAK

The young child in our midst is often treated from the parental or caretaker perspective. And while it is good and fitting that parts of the worship service speak to the child, much of this standard fare is condescending. The impression is always given that adults are there to look after the child until he or she grows to the one acceptable state of Christian faith and life: adulthood. It is only when the person attains adulthood that he or she is seriously considered to be a contributing member of the faith community.

Many books have been written about the church's ministry *to* children. Some have been written about the church's ministry *with* children. The radical thrust of this book is its focus on the ministry *of* children.

The authors have long been accustomed to the notion that children need the church. We now assert that the church desperately needs the children. In saying this, we are not propounding a gospel of children. However, we are saying that the gospel cannot be understood without deliberate openness to the child spirit. This encounter with the spirit of the child within us can best be enabled in relationship with natural Starchildren: the children and babies within our families, church, and community.

Our personal spiritual nurture is largely dependent upon the ministry of children to us. We need the child in order to be whole. At the same time, the child needs the adult.

The authors are convinced that Jesus was serious when he said that childlike qualities are keys to the Kingdom. Children are put among us in order that they might minister to the church. The child needs the adult to enable him or her to express and celebrate these Starchild qualities.

We are not employing the term *Starchildren* in the sense of science fiction or fantasy. It is the star of Bethlehem that sparks our imagination and vision. The advent of the Christ shakes the boundaries of all our previous understanding.

Starchildren are not fictional creatures from another time and space. They are our children, our toddlers, our babies. They are of us and yet are beyond us.

We see glimpses of ourselves in their faces and their actions. But there is something more. Their openness, their gentleness, their spontaneity, are of a different order from that which surrounds them. We adults routinely seek to disguise and/or hide our need for personal love. Babies and toddlers seek it with shameless determination.

Where do these "other" qualities come from? Certainly not entirely from us. Our children are also children of the universe. They come to us red-hot from the heart of God. For this reason, the authors name them Starchildren.

But Starchildren are not only the very young. The Starchild quality is something eternal. That is, it exists within the psyche of every person. But too frequently the Starchild within an adult is fettered by inhibitions and is made impotent by violent wounding. Nonetheless, the Starchild within is never so scarred that he or she cannot live again. The authors believe that Jesus was alluding to this very resurrection when he talked of "being born again."

The Starchild spirit is available to every child of God—regardless of age. Our babies and young children have these gifts in abundance. It is these infants that can lead us to celebration of the child within us all.

The authors are not psychologists or child-development experts. But in the last few years it has just happened that children have led us and taught us. We feel we have been born anew and have become Starchildren. We want to share our personal testimony and put forward our hunches about ways local congregations and individuals might experience a similar awakening.

Many folk have helped us plow this rich ground. The typing of Marion Renn and Sandra McNulty have pushed this project into existence under very trying circumstances. Anne Merrifield, extraordinary enabler of children, has helped us in many ways. We are especially indebted to the Ringwood parish of the Uniting Church in Australia for encouraging Stan to commit himself to this project.

The authors have drawn inspiration and vision from the sensitive and creative ministry of Fred Rogers. For both of us, he has been the medium and the message of being with children.

Wives Lois and Marilyn are special for special reasons. Their love and faith have helped us grow young. And children Michelle, James, Amy, Cathy, and Jill have effectively converted us. They daily transform us into children through their invitation to play.

The Starchildren who peek out from these pages are real. We simply pass along their stories. They have teased, loved, forgiven, and helped us feel what it is to be alive again to the profound simplicity of Christ.

Some Basic Assumptions

The authors have certain prejudices that soon come to the surface. These assumptions mold the shape of this book.
1. The childlike quality underscored in the gospel is the key to faith and life.
2. Babies, toddlers, and young children have been naturally granted the quality needed by the church if it is to be faithful to its true essence. If acknowledged and valued, Starchildren can help enable the community of faith to be whole.
3. Starchildren are those of any age who permit the spirit

of God to lead them to become "as little children," again and again.

4. The time is right to affirm strongly that the Starchild has a unique ministry to individuals, the church, and the society.

5. Starchildren need the care of adults if they are to survive; adults need the care of Starchildren if they are to grow.

Mind Maps for Reading The Ministry of the Child

There are probably many ways to get into this book. There is no "right" or "authorized" method of approaching it. We encourage readers to find the way that is right for them. But in case you want some guideposts, here are a few of the ways this book can be read.

As an anthology of stories about children. There are lots of them, and all of them are true.

As a list of personal expositions about the place of children in the church and in the lives of individuals. These expositions cut across the generations and touch many of the recurring questions of life.

As a study book for a six-week course or weekend retreat. For this use there is study-guide material in the back.

As the basis of a course for the parents or families of newly baptized/dedicated children. There is a user's guide in the back of the book with helpful ideas.

As the preparation necessary for an "all-age celebration." Suggestions for such a celebration are included in the back of the book.

No matter how you do it, we know that to you the views of the authors are not important. The critical thing is what you think and feel within. It is this that will decide if the child in your family, on your street, in your church, or in your heart lives free or shackled in chains.

We have shared something of our own inner dynamics. We do this in the hope of sparking dialogue. As Starchildren have begun to speak to us, so we hope and pray that the Starchildren around and within you will be both seen and heard. If this book helps make possible that process, we will rejoice.

PROPOSITION 1

STARCHILDREN ARE THE MOST IMMEDIATE ACCESS TO GOD'S GENEROSITY.

Small Change

"I would like to make a donation." The voice seemed to come from nowhere. My head was deep in the trunk of the car. Turning, I saw a small boy standing behind me. In his hand he held a small spring-lock coin holder. He extended it toward me.

"I would like to make a donation," he repeated.

"To me?" I questioned.

"No," he said, "to the church. How can I do that?"

"Well," I replied, "I guess you'll have to wait until they take up the offering, and that will be quite awhile." The boy looked disappointed.

I hurried on with the unloading task. I was preoccupied. Lots of things can go wrong when you're preaching with the help of media and especially when you're a stranger in a strange land.

"Do you want to see how this works?" the boy asked. He held the coin holder close to my face. I nodded my assent. He began to slide the money out of the holder.

"I just got it this week." There was pleasure and pride in his voice. He watched me withdraw and then replace the money in the holder.

"What's your name?" I asked.

"Wayne. What's yours?"

"Stan," I replied.

Once inside the hall I received the greeting appropriate for an out-of-state speaker. Once they had laden me with sandwiches and coffee, the good folk of the church left me to my own devices. I sat alone. The sounds of fellowship filled the hall. Wayne, with two other nine-year-old boys in tow, joined me.

"Do you think it will be long now?" he asked. In his hand he clutched the coin holder, jammed with silver coins.

"I'm sure they won't take up the offering till a later time," I replied. "Haven't you seen them do it before?"

"Oh, I've only been coming here for three weeks," he confided. "My mom and brother are over there." He pointed to a pretty woman and a small replica of himself sitting close beside her. "We started coming to church when my dad left home. I wish my dad were home." His face became clouded.

"Do you ever see your dad now?" I inquired.

"Yes, every Saturday. I know where he lives, but I can't sleep at his house." His eyes were sad.

After these revelations, Wayne obviously felt it was time to change the subject. He politely asked about my home and family. He searched the table for cakes, took one himself, and offered me the choice of the remainder. The cakes I declined, but I affirmed that I had certainly enjoyed being a part of Wayne's circle. Wayne and his friends had helped me through what could have been a very unfriendly fellowship tea.

As guest preacher, I was led to the grand isolation of a front pew. Seeing that once again I was left quite alone, Wayne and friends came to sit beside me. Wayne sat there fingering his coin holder. For the tenth time he told me he just couldn't wait to make his donation.

The minister called on me to pray. On my return to the seat, Wayne pulled my coat sleeve. He whispered in my ear, "Pretty good prayer, Stan." I was touched and strangely flattered. I wasn't used to anyone's saying anything about my prayers.

Wayne was not caught up in the hymns. He obviously felt that the singing of the hymns provided convenient interludes during which he could move from the front to the back pew where his mother was sitting. Would you believe, when the time for the offering finally came, Wayne was not sitting beside me? I was disappointed. I would not witness the long-awaited donation.

One of Wayne's young friends had not deserted me. As the offering steward moved toward us, my young friend showed signs of restlessness. He was looking hard at the offering I held in my hand. It dawned on me that he didn't have an offering. I felt through my pockets for a solution, but there was none there that I could find.

"Stan, may I put in your offering?" The question took me back. But I could think of no respectable reason why not. As the offering plate approached us, I was conscious of my empty-handedness. But I need not have worried.

For when the time came to make his offering my friend informed the offering steward, "It's from him." The steward smiled. I was strangely moved. Once again a child had taken me by surprise.

Wayne returned to our pew during the next hymn. In his hand he clutched the now-empty coin holder. For a minute or so he was completely engrossed by the offering plate that set in plain view on the Communion table. He leaned toward me. "How much do you reckon we got?" he asked.

After the service there were hands to shake and greetings to exchange. Finally there was nothing left to do but pack up my equipment. At the front of the sanctuary the church treasurer was intent on counting the offering. The contents of the bowl were scattered over the Communion table. He was not on his own. Wayne was there engrossed in the counting. As I passed the table I heard Wayne ask, "Can I count the dimes?" The treasurer was not enjoying the attention of his young, would-be assistant, but Wayne continued to offer help. The treasurer finally grumbled something about not needing any help. Wayne gave a little shrug and left him.

"Stan, I want you to have this." Wayne stood before me. In his outstretched hand he held his beloved coin holder. At first I thought he might be joking.

"Stan, I want you to have it." His eyes were serious. Uneasiness stirred within me. Wayne waited. That strange little object was of no value to me but of great value to him. Yet Wayne wanted to give it to me. It made no sense to me at all.

"Wayne," I said, "that's terrific of you to offer it to me, but I can't accept it. I know how much it means to you." Wayne did not withdraw his hand.

"I want you to have it, Stan." I was somewhere between embarrassed and offended. Clichés about taking candy from kids clogged my mind. I gave him a rough hug and said a very firm, "No, thanks." Wayne left.

A few minutes later he was back. He stood between me and the door. There was no way I could miss him. His hand was held out. The silver coin holder glistened. "I'd like you to have it." I was taken back by his persistence. Once again I refused. As carefully as I could I explained that it would really be of more use to him than it ever would be to me. He seemed to accept my point. I continued to pack up the remainder of my equipment, but I was troubled.

Inside the hall Wayne was standing by his mother. She talked earnestly to the minister. Seeing me enter, Wayne took a few steps down the aisle in my direction. I waved.

Encouraged by my response, he came to me. He raised one hand in a kind of salute. Between his fingers I could see the shape of the silver coin holder. Suddenly I knew I had to take it.

"Wayne, I'll tell you what, I'll swap you." Relieved, Wayne immediately pushed the object into my hand.

"You don't have to swap me. I just want you to have it." I explained that it would make me feel better to swap.

In the car park, Wayne stood beside me as I searched through my bags looking for my supply of children's books. I couldn't find a thing. I felt very uncomfortable; I just had to find something to give this child. At last I uncovered a child's book. It was one of those "helping children to cope" books with the unlikely title of *The Day Grandma Died.* Wayne was not too impressed. He wasn't very interested in that kind of thing, he said. Nonetheless, I suspect for my sake, he kept the book.

Wayne and I live thousands of miles apart. His little coin holder lives in the pocket of my suit. I have never used it to hold change. Whenever my fingers touch its surface, I think of Wayne. And that's just what he wanted me to do.

EXPOSITION

Christ calls his people to transform hostility into hospitality. Consequently, being friendly is a concept so central to the Christian faith that it is simply not respectable for a Christian to be anything else. The leaders of most sophisticated congregations are likely to tremble in their shoes at the slightest suggestion that theirs is an unfriendly church.

So it is that in one way or another, every congregation is concerned about the practice of hospitality. For instance, most congregations will offer words of welcome to the stranger and be sure his coffee cup is full. However, these things are outward forms of hospitality. If that is all that is offered, then the stranger will remain a stranger.

Hospitality has other essential components. Children, toddlers, and babies are naturals when it comes to the practice of these facets of hospitality. They instinctively know how to make a person feel welcome. They offer strangers unconditional acceptance, the warmth of their smiles, and participation in their enjoyment of that moment.

Wayne and his friends chose their pieces of cake before offering any to me. This is out of step with the etiquette of hospitality. But what they did share was of much greater worth. They welcomed me into their lives. A feeling of at-homeness is dependent on welcomes like that.

Children Feel

It is not natural for an unprovoked child to want to hurt or embarrass another person. That is not to say that children do not do such things. However, such hurting behavior is always learned from something or someone in their environment.

Children are sensitive. They are able to sense pain and discomfort in others. Given the opportunity, they will support and encourage those around them. With children, especially small children, there is consistency between the medium and the message. Consequently, their ways of communicating encouragement and support are childlike. Often, adults label children's supportive communications as quaint or amusing and so dismiss them. To do this is to miss the point and the power of the child's support.

Our children are willing to do all within their power to help us. To accept this help is to place oneself within the field of an energy source of great significance.

Repeating Signals

We sometimes talk as though a characteristic of childhood is impatience. In fact, the exact opposite is the case. Teens and adults are frequently impatient. Our Starchildren come to us with the patience of Job. Without this patience, this ability to be content for long periods with simple things, they would never learn, never grow. Like many other Starchild qualities, this gift is easily and quickly subverted.

The child displays this quality of patience not only in receiving information but also in his or her transmission of signals. When something is happening deep within the child, he or she will try to communicate the essence of these concerns. What they lack in descriptive skills, our children make up in patience. Again and again they will try to tell us what is in their hearts. With a child it is never a case of "get this the first time, or I won't tell you again." Children keep transmitting their essential messages in as many ways as they can. They live in the hope that "next time I will be understood."

Beware, however, for there is an end to this patience. If unheeded and unheard the child will eventually give up. This giving up leads to the hiding of feelings, at which the adult world is so adept. This retreat from communication leads away from the life-giving qualities with which the Starchild is equipped at birth.

Paying for Services

We feel good when we give things to children. As their eyes light up with gratitude, we feel big. As donors we are relaxed and at ease.

Receiving from children is a horse of a completely different color. It's not so bad when children give to us gifts they have bought with money we have given them or gifts they have made. This kind of gift-receiving is pleasant and nonthreatening.

The problem with children as givers is that they do not seem to know where to draw the line. If we allow them, their giving will go far beyond reasonable generosity into the realm of plain foolishness.

Life has taught the rest of us to hold our precious things close, to confine our gift-giving to what we can afford, those things we can do without. In stark contrast to this, children are likely to give away their most precious things. To those who have made measured generosity a principle of life, the unconsidered generosity of children can be quite unnerving.

As we grow, the idea that our children are indebted to us grows also. Once this mind-set is established, we are unable to live comfortably with the idea that we are indebted to our children. Confronted with the generosity of our Starchildren, we struggle to find ways to pay them off. Our aim is to maintain our one-up status.

And why not? After all, of what value are the trinkets of children to us? At the most, they may be symbols of love, at the least, reminders that our children care for us. Who needs such symbols? Of what possible use can such reminders be to us? After all, it is common knowledge that our children must have our love to survive, and as for our needs, well—

PROPOSITION 2

THE GIFT OF AWE IS OFFERED TO THE FAITH COMMUNITY THROUGH THE MINISTRY OF STARCHILDREN!

Amy and Jill and—

Awe and wonder: "Daddy, Daddy, Daddy!" These cries always sent me through the ceiling because they always came in the middle of the night. When my heart settled a bit, I would see Amy or Jill standing next to the bed. "Spider!" The word was conveyed with the appropriate emphasis to send chills down my spine. The spider stage hit the girls at different times. However, I knew the fear that strangled their world at that moment. For them, every section of wall in the dark bedroom concealed hairy-legged monsters.

It was during Amy's spider phase that I finally hit upon a strategy to combat the loathsome creatures of the dark. One night I carried my frightened daughter back to her room. Our careful examination of the room did nothing to alleviate the terror. I finally stepped into the hall and fetched a can of room disinfectant spray. "This is the magical spray. It will chase away all spiders and monsters of the night." The odor of the spray filled our nostrils. Amy's eyes carefully scanned the yellow container. There was wonder and awe in the power of this small can. She settled down in her bed and was soon fast asleep.

Awe and wonder: I can still remember the burning eyes of the nun. She was strong and mysterious. Did she really have legs like Mother? Or did her long black skirts hide wooden posts? The eyes of five-year-olds tend to become trapped by all kinds of mysteries. We also were awed by our visits to the church. Each week the nuns took us from the school we attended into the darkened sanctuary. The stained-glass windows, the strange odors, and the stations of the cross were overwhelming. Sister Rita would stoop over us with her black robes, looking a bit like the wicked witch in Walt Disney's production of *Snow White* and hiss at us, "Sit here. I have to turn on the light." Every five-year-old head would spin toward the light. We focused on that spot on the wall until we were about to explode. I could feel my heart beating as Sister disappeared. "She is going to get J-E-S-U-S!" We resented Mark's statement of the obvious. We had decided long ago that "J-E-S-U-S" was on his way. Then a huge red glow flashed out from the wall like a flame of fire. We fell back in the pews. God had arrived!

I haven't often experienced such awe and wonder since those mysterious Friday-morning moments in that church. I shouldn't have returned to the building a couple of years ago. It was a bit disappointing to discover that an Exit sign had taken the place of God's special landing light.

Closed Communion: Scott rolls and twists in the pew. He is not being restless or bad. In fact, this nine-year-old is one of the most serious Christians I have ever met. He loves being with me. When someone loves Christ with all his little heart, then ministers have to be special. This is a bad Sunday for my small friend. Instead of being a high point in the life of our congregation, it will be a day of tears and sadness. I will be sad, but Scott will shed tears. It is Communion Sunday, and this church does not welcome children to the Lord's table. His mother and father will taste and see how good God is in this great act of celebration.

Scott will not be comforted. "I love Jesus. I want to be the closest to him."

The young boy stands beside me as I clean up after the service. I touch his shoulder. He looks at me. I take a piece of bread and dip it into the juice. "Take, eat, Scott. This is the body and blood of Jesus who loves you." His chin trembles. His eyes widen in awe. I place the elements in his mouth, and he chews slowly. The wonder and awe welled up so completely within his heart are now fulfilled. He knows that Christ loves him and that he and his Lord are one.

Unfortunately the last paragraph didn't happen. It is true that Scott cried and twisted in the pew every time we celebrated the enacted Word. This Starchild was longing to fuse our worship with the kind of faith no longer alive within most of the acceptable guests at the Lord's table. We made him wait. We knew the rules of the church. It is good adult theology that we wear like a coat of mail. Scott is not in the church today. It is strange. His awe and wonder are now directed somewhere else. We didn't lose Scott. We lost.

Eye of the beholder: The camera rolls in for a close-up. The eyes of the five-year-old child widen. He sees something that brings a look of expectation and wonder to his face. You know that he is going to leap forth and embrace what he must behold more closely. Suddenly the arms of his mother lasso his neck and torso. She is dragging him back. He fights against her protective hold. The room suddenly explodes with light and heat energy. The sound envelopes every-thing with a shrieking madness that threatens to destroy the house. There is some alien force probing the country farm. The mother knows that she must protect her babe from the unspeakable unknown. He breaks free and rushes through the small passage into the arms of this unseen force. The last glimpse of his face shows pure wonder and joy. The child recognizes the benevolent qualities of this encounter.

The late seventies will best be remembered by mass media magnates as the revolution of wonder flicks. George Lucas and his film-making kin blitzed the media world and shook the movie financial community. The films opened star worlds and close encounters neglected by every other facet of our culture. The educational, political, and religious wells were overflowing with pessimistic technological systems. At the very moment when the church had demythologized angels and the government had lapsed into zero budgeting (start with nothing and plan accordingly), the film arts challenged the imagination of the mass audience.

Martin Marty reminded an assembly of youth workers in Chicago that religion begins with wonder. However, where do we find the experience of awe within the celebration of the faith community in the local setting? It rarely emerges at church suppers, during stewardship campaigns, or even in worship events. Religious folk often claim that they can only glimpse the ground-shaking encounter with the wonder and awe in strange pockets of celebration. Some seek spirit-filled splinter groups or individual highs in the latest sect gathering.

There was a time when the foundations of life were shaken by the power of the Christ event. The awe and wonder of the Bethlehem stable, the hillside storytelling, and a stark cross once generated excitement and awe whenever the people gathered. The Word was preached and enacted, and then the people went forth to serve. This is simply not the case today.

Again, it is the ministry of the Starchildren that can renew the awe and wonder of faith that is ours through the birth, ministry, death, and resurrection of Jesus Christ. The young/old Starchildren are grasped by micromoments of awe and wonder. The majesty and power of God are known through the beauty of an unfolding rose or a wriggling worm. The Starchild within us struggles to escape our cultural prisons and embrace the life around us. Yet the social cloak adults wear restrains such temptation.

The soloist ends the hymn she has so beautifully shared with the small congregation. There are tears in her eyes. Everyone is moved by the sheer wonder and awe of God's message breaking forth at this time and place and in this person. Yet everyone feels uncomfortable. People work to stifle the watery eyes and the lump in their throat. A small child breaks the silence with the sound of clapping hands. He is bobbing up and down with great glee.

We are imprisoned and drugged by the sophistication and coolness of the world around us. The systems and principalities force the Starchild within us to hide—and die. Yet God is known to us only through his awe and wonder. It is the Starchild who can lead us to celebrate this power and hope.

PROPOSITION 3

STARCHILDREN ARE THE HEALING HANDS OF CHRIST.

Healing Touch

"They have found lumps in my body," she said. "The results of the tests will be known on Tuesday." Her voice trembled as she spoke. I knew she suspected the worst. Frankly, so did I. For months she had been looking unwell. From my figuring, she could be little more than fifty. She looked much older than that. After I prayed, there were tears in her eyes. They were in mine also. I hoped she did not notice.

I worked late into the night on Saturday. Searching for the right text, the right prayers, the right words. Usually I try not to prepare services around the needs of just one person, but this was different. Besides, we all face suffering, and who knows how close death is to any one of us? Tomorrow I'd have to face her sitting there, fourth row from the front. She would be there looking for a word from the Lord, a word of comfort, a word to sustain her until Tuesday and beyond. My God, how I searched for that word.

Sometimes, the more you prepare, the worse it gets. Well, that Sunday the worship was heavy. The fine phrases didn't flow, the warmth I so much wished to project seemed to have evaporated. She sat there gaunt and shriveled. Going by the look in her eyes, she had already received her death sentence. My theme was "hope," but I really felt as though I were pronouncing the last rites.

As I ponderously launched into my third point, a small toddler left his parents in a pew toward the back and made his way down the aisle. At the fourth row from the front he paused, turned, and climbed on the seat. He sat there beside her. I don't think he said anything, just snuggled in. Her arm encircled him. He responded with a hug. He sat with her for only a minute or so, and then he went back to his parents. But, my God, her face! I saw it. Warmth and hope once again lived in her eyes, courage shone in her bearing. She had received her gospel for the day.

No one else in the congregation could have seen what I saw. So no one else really understood why her face was so bright at the end of the service. Some of the more pious among us noted that she had apparently been blessed. Indeed, she had. In the house of God, during the hour of worship, she had been hugged by a small child.

As I walked home, I thought about the way we used to do things. The way we used to insist that children sit with their parents and never move. We used to argue that any movement would be distracting and would interrupt our communication with the Almighty. I tried to think why we did that. I suppose it was because we presumed that messages from God could come only through the pulpit. I thought about her. "The service was such a help," she said. I knew why, and I thanked God.

EXPOSITION

I used to look forward to the time when the children left the worship service. Praying and preaching were always much easier in congregations without children. Adults do not interrupt. And they give the impression at least that they are paying attention. Children get in the way of this one-way flow of information and inspiration.

That's how I used to think. When I was converted and started to think of children as real people, as real members of the Body of Christ, I began to wonder what they could contribute. That was a hard question. I had always thought in terms of what the Body has to give to them. But Paul does speak as though every member, even the little members, have special work to do to make the Body go and grow. But, except for crying out loud, what can children, babies, and toddlers give to the church?

I am still working on that one, but at least now I have a few clues. The first thing that came to me had to do with the nature of the church. I reasoned that if children were part of the church, they ought to be with us in worship. Sounds like a good idea, but I was left with the question, What could they get out of worship? I was not even ready to face the question, What could they give to it? However, the conviction grew within me that they ought to be there. That is how I began in faith to encourage the children, toddlers, and babies to stay throughout worship.

They made their presence felt. They cried, they talked, they walked, they ran. At first, I was irritated, annoyed, and disoriented; and so was the congregation. However, with surprising speed we learned to cope with one another. And there were better things in store because the children began to contribute to our worship life.

The comfortable acceptance of the children in worship began in me with a change of heart. I forced myself to think of the children not as emissaries of the devil sent to destroy our worship but as messengers from God sent to help us. This meant I began to search for anything of value that their presence contributed to the worship.

A startling thought dawned on me: Could it be that the contributions of our smallest members were their interruptions? Was it possible that their movements and noises were somehow aids to worship? Following this line of thought, I

31

began to ponder what message could be contained in their interruptions. Well, I've thought of some.

Church folk and ministers object to interruptions by children because they disrupt the flow of liturgy and intrude on the preaching. We proceed with services of worship in somber tones and high seriousness. We have developed this art of divine worship to perfection. But let us never forget that we lack indisputable confirmation that God shares our opinion. Who says what we are saying and doing is so good and right, anyway?

As every leader of worship knows, children are just as likely to interrupt at the highest and holiest moment as any other. Perhaps this is not such a bad thing. Leaders of religious ceremonies are constantly tempted to take themselves and the liturgies too seriously. It was so in Jesus' day; so it is today. Could it not be that our children are sent by God to prick the balloons of our pomposity?

To begin to listen for a word from the Lord in the interruptions of children requires a change of heart in most worship leaders and most congregations. Minister and congregation must be willing to smile at themselves and see their liturgies as imperfect vehicles. They must be willing to stop, look, and listen to the current of divine life that flows into worship when there is a welcome for Starchildren.

When this is done, worship will take on a new spirit and a new feel. It may move down the previous liturgical trail, but it will do so at a different rhythm. And all this is not the result of some upbeat liturgical design but simply the dynamic the children bring with them. Worship becomes more vital and certainly more spontaneous. It takes on a feel unlike any other human gathering. That is the point.

Body Language

Children talk with their whole selves. What they lack in vocabulary, they make up for in gesture, expression, touch, and feel. Babies and toddlers cling to us, sit on us, lie on us, wrap themselves around our legs, hold our hands, and kiss our faces. All these things they do without training or coaching. To Starchildren it is just a natural way to be.

This is not to say that this mode of behavior cannot be soon thwarted, rerouted, or even eliminated. It can be done but not easily nor quickly. It can be observed that children from environments where there has been little show of outward affection will quickly establish hugging ways given half a chance. Also, it is a fact that some children are by temperament demonstrative and others not. Nonetheless, the assertion stands: All children want to express their love in physical modes. Body language is never so important as when you are small.

When properly understood, the body communication of our Starchildren is a means of grace.

To anxious persons in what seems like a hostile world, the touch of a child is reassuring and calming.

To guilty persons bearing loads of condemnation from without or within, the hug of a child can be a fanfare of reprieve.

To lonely and frightened people, the warmth of a child's body is a welcome back into the human race, a bright invitation to hope.

Think for a minute what all this might mean if acknowledged and welcomed within the circle of the Christian church. After all, congregations are commissioned by Christ to bind up wounds, to heal, to reconcile, and to forgive. And how do they do this? The most usual way in which local congregations approach these tasks is to sing hymns with appropriate lyrics and to talk and pray about them. That is, they use the verbal approach. All this may sound good, and certainly it's safe and unthreatening. But how effective are words in binding up the bleeding spirits of wounded people?

When a congregation welcomes its children into worship and sets them free to relate to the whole church, they are clearing the way for the inclusion of the body language of Starchildren in worship. As the children feel at home and move among the congregation, they will take their body language with them. Small children and toddlers just don't sit next to people, they lean on them. They look for hugs and are glad to hold hands. They may bestow the blessing of their company only for a minute or so, but what meaning those minutes may contain!

As we gather for worship, we do so in the hope that we may praise God and be touched by him. For some strange reason we have thought this can only be done in words. The Starchildren of the congregation can be, for some who sorely need it, the incarnation of that divine touch of healing and wholeness. The fact that our children are unaware that they bring with them such a important element of worship is as it should be. They will know that they are welcome and valued, and that is enough for them. On the other hand, if our liturgies or frame of mind prevents this healing ministry's happening, then that's a congregational tragedy. The blighting effects of this tragedy will touch all sections of the church.

PROPOSITION 4

THOSE
WHO NURTURE STARCHILDREN
ARE THEMSELVES NURTURED.

Close Encounter

It's one thing to have an idea; it's another thing to make that idea work—particularly when the idea affects the well-being of many other people. That was precisely my problem.

For a few weeks I had been encouraging the congregation to keep the children in worship. Parents were skeptical, middle-aged folk a little on edge; but no one actually spoke out against the idea. So at first one, then two brave families had their children stay with them throughout the worship hour. You can guess what happened.

When the first few tiny tots came rocking down the aisle, I thought I would try a pretend-they're-not-there strategy. I even kept up this charade as two of them swung on the Communion table. I preached louder and made more hand movements. It was a hopeless cause. I now know that no sermon in the world stands a chance against a child's swinging on the Communion table.

For me it was a moment of truth. I was tense and distracted. At first the congregation was amused but not for long. The I-told-you-so people were in their glory. The hopefuls whom I had been able to enthuse were clearly shaken. I had to either abandon the idea or develop some strategies for coping.

A number of things happened, and some I made to happen. For me one thing was internal. I began searching my head for the possible meaning of the children's interruptions. Could it be they were some kind of contribution? This line of thought proved to be most helpful.

My spirit relaxed within me. I was able to go with the flow. I no longer pretended that the little people weren't there. I was able to smile at their meanderings and to enjoy their unselfconscious explorations. Nothing was so high-powered or important that it could not pause while a small child occupied the attention of the congregation. My attitude was picked up by the congregation, and this helped them relax. My attitude was especially helpful to the parents. The interruptions of their children were accept-able. They were not destroying our God relationship. It was OK to enjoy them after all.

But, there was one little three-year-old who didn't know when enough was enough. Swinging on the table one Sunday was followed by climbing on it the next. I began to wonder what that tiny tot would do for an encore. I was sure he felt a pull toward a life in the circus. Clearly, he was mistaking our sanctuary for a sawdust circle. He had to be stopped.

This is how it happened. I saw him coming, rolling down the aisle, all energy and good nature. His mother up the back had lowered her eyes; I suspect she didn't care to watch. I knew and everyone else knew that he was making for the Communion table. The spirit moved me and I moved.

I left the pulpit and moved into the center aisle. I stood between him and the Communion table. He grinned and looked up at me. It wasn't easy, but I summoned a smile and crouched down. Our eyes met on a horizontal plane.

I was suddenly aware of a deafening silence. Glancing up, I could see that the children in the second row were standing up. The atmosphere was like high noon at the O.K. corral. The whole congregation seemed to be holding its breath.

He was taken aback for a minute, then, deciding it was a game, moved to pass me on the left. I put my hand on his arm. Words came to me, and by the grace of God I said something like this: "Hey, we are so glad that you're here with us, and it's terrific that you feel free enough to move around. But look, there's something you should know. Look around. Do you notice how everyone else is sitting still?" He nodded. "Do you know why?" He shook his head. "It is because we are all trying to listen to God. Hey, do you know what? If you move around too much, you might make it difficult for them to hear him." He seemed to be listening hard. Certainly everyone else in the church was. "See, this isn't a kindergarten playground. When you move around, why don't you do it really quietly and mainly up the back."

He stared at me. The church was very quiet. In one salvo, I had fired off all my shots. If they didn't take effect, I was dead. I took my hand from his arm, and after a moment of indecision, he flashed me a big smile and turned around and toddled back to his mother. I lived.

Believe it or not, that was the start of a very special friendship. Over the next couple of months, he came to the front on several occasions. Always it was to intercept some other wayward toddler. Firmly he would take them by the hand and lead them toward the back of the church. As far as I know, no one asked him to do it. He seemed to feel that it was his responsibility. And I got the feeling he was doing it for me.

EXPOSITION

Many times we talk to parents about children when we would do much better talking directly to the children themselves. This applies not only to teen-agers and older children but also to preschoolers and younger. As a matter of fact, in a number of situations with supposedly difficult children, I have found it to be the only way to go. Many times the parents have given up; and yet when they are respectfully spoken to by some other adult, new patterns of behavior emerge.

To be taken seriously by the child, we must first be able to demonstrate that we are taking him or her seriously. Using threats and laying on guilt will not be effective in gaining the active cooperation of our children. On the other hand, respect, explanations, and dialogue through continuing friendship can work wonders!

Here is a basic premise from which I work. The child is not against us, he is for us. He does not want to break up our hearts, our spirits, or our worship. Actually, our children want to help us if only they can find a way to do this. Working on this premise, I approach children in hope, and this hope seldom has been disappointed.

The direct-talking style recommended here is a method I have used on several occasions. When telling of my approach to this type of situation, it often becomes clear that my audience suspects that this way of doing things will be offensive to parents. I have not found it to be so. On the contrary, parents are glad that someone else takes a hand in helping their child fit in to worship. On the other hand, the "scowling and growling" method of dealing with noisy children in church is, I believe, highly offensive to both children and parents.

There are a couple of other things I do to help win the cooperation of very active children. One is that I make particular friendship with these little people. Before and after the service, I take the opportunity to share part of myself with them and learn from them about the interesting things in their lives. We quickly become pals. Pals generally want to help one another, and that's just what they do.

For some years now we have let it be known to our smallest children that it is OK to move around during worship. However, as can be seen from the above situation, we do suggest certain limits. But the practice of visiting with adults other than blood family is seen as a good thing to do. Further, should the small child wish to sit with a number of adults in the course of one worship service, there are no problems. In the context of worship, my aim is not to build blood-family solidarity but Christian, extended-family solidarity. The latter is a much more significant sign of what Christ would do with his people. The sharing of children within the congregation is a unique sign that the spirit of the living Christ is in the midst. Also, it allows a whole new possibility in interpersonal ministries (see "Healing Touch," p. 29).

Another approach that has been most helpful has been the creation of a concept known as "Crèche in the Corner." This is in fact a small area at the back of the sanctuary that is carpeted and equipped with soft toys, books, and crayons. In my present church, where fixed pews prevent this arrangement, the back portion of the center aisle has proved to be entirely satisfactory. Children are welcome to use the equipment in this area. However, it is important to note that this facility is only used during the second half of worship service or during the period of the sermon.

PROPOSITION 5

THE FINGER OF GOD CAN BE FELT
IN THE TOUCH OF A CHILD'S HAND.

Mother's Touch and—

The huge door slammed shut. The click of the lock struck terror in the heart of the small child. He struggled at the door knob. It was useless for the two-year-old. "Mamma, Mamma, Mamma!" The cries echoed down the hallway of the duplex. The child knew that he would never see his mother again. Fortunately, such fears were mere exaggerations in the terror-strickened mind of the small boy.

My mother quickly found her trapped son who had wandered off. She could hear my frightened screams through the solid door. "Push your fingers out here, son." She wedged her fingers under the door. She could feel my tiny fingers. I thrust them through the crack and found the rush of comfort as I felt my mother's touch.

Years later she would tell me how good it was to feel her young son's fingers. I quickly stopped my screaming. My tears were soothed into sniffles until I was rescued by the building superintendent with his master key.

Years later I would stand in the operating room of a children's hospital and hold the pacifier and fingertips of another small child. This dear baby gripped my gloved finger. The doctors were trying to perform a miracle operation to save the tiny life that was slipping away. "We can't give her much to put her under. Each bit that cuts off the pain also kills her a little."

Fortunately, such babies don't feel pain in the same way it is experienced by adults. She fell off into unconsciousness as they probed away at her infected stomach. I will never forget the grasp on me. Finally, tiny fingers slipped away from my large hand. So did her life.

Anne was a striking fifteen-year-old. It wasn't beauty or style that made her stand out among the eighty high school young people at the retreat. Her body was carried in a protective manner that did not invite physical contact. She seemed to enwrap herself in her arms. Anne was a rock; she was an island.

The weekend was one those special happenings. Strangers came from different places to be a family of love and faith. Part of the spiritual journey came through hours of talk and sharing afforded by the event. Late Saturday night Anne and I finally had a chance to talk. It was she who approached me. As we talked, bridges began to form between us. It was 2:00 A.M. We continued to talk. "My dad left my mother. I am glad. He used to abuse me. He—forced me—to—have sex with him." Tears rolled down her cheeks. She pulled her knees under her chin and wrapped her arms around herself like a hermit crab retreating into its shell. I wanted to reach out and comfort her. She sensed my care and natural reactions. "Don't touch me! I will never let anybody touch me!" Finally, she accepted my assurance that I would not touch her.

"I am out of touch with everything. I don't belong anywhere. I wish I were a child. Then someone could cuddle me and make me feel safe."

The next day the whole group moved through a beautiful two-hour worship celebration. We were linked together by a long rope. Then the rope was cut into sections. We tied the pieces of rope on one another's wrist. At the end of the amazing service we could feel the power of Christ flowing through us. We were close as parts of the Body of Christ. People naturally embraced and passed the peace of Christ.

Anne stood in the middle of the circling mass of loving sisters and brothers. She slowly moved toward me. Her hands reach out and tied the piece of rope on my wrist. I also tied the bracelet on her wrist. There were tears in her eyes. Yet the nature of her stare was much different from what I had seen the night before. There was no fear. She had the gaze of a trusting child. I smiled. She threw her arms around me and hugged me. I couldn't keep back my tears. In a special way she had become a child again.

Burns are ugly and are the cause of much concern for those treating them. Eddie was a delightful baby. Yet, the raw flesh brought pain to every adult who saw the wounds. There would be years of skin grafts for this small child. It had been an accident beyond the scope of his parents' protection. It happened so fast. In his natural exploration of life, Eddie had reached out to touch the shiny coffee maker. The twelve cups of scalding liquid had poured over his near-nude body. In his lust for growth and exploration, he had to let his touch guide him into a new realm, a realm of suffering.

It is tattered and ripped. The color has faded and the material is worn away. Nine years is a long time for a baby's blanket. Yet the wear from countless nights of stroking and touch makes it ever more dear to Jill. This is her special "blankie." Its touch has carried her through all kinds of pain and joy. The fear of the next day's dental appointment and the anticipation of Christmas morning have both been awaited with good ole blankie. There is something so supportive in feeling the familiar.

The child weaves dangerously back and forth in the arms of her mother. She is facing the stranger. Maggie yearns to explore the surface of the new face before her. She reaches out and runs her fingertips through the beard on the face of the man. A smile explodes on her face. She reaches out and touches it again. This time she whips her head around and casts her giggles of pleasure at her mother.

EXPOSITION

The blind, deaf, and dumb kid in the rock musical *Tommy* by the Who offers the challenge of the ages when he pleads for someone to touch him, feel him, and heal him. It is legend in most hospitals that certain doctors have "the touch." They seem to be healers who can add to the natural strength of the patient by their mere presence or touch.

The early church appreciated the power in the touch of faith. Healings, rebukes, commissioning, and loving were occasions when flesh touched flesh. Yet what seems so natural and desirable in the world of the biblical times and of childhood is dampened in contemporary faith life. The man in the next pew may be trembling with fear, his knuckles white with tension when the passing of peace is encouraged. Yet Christ invites Tommy and all the rest of us to put our hands into the very wounds of his body.

It is the Starchild who can lead us back to the touch of faith. The power of this tiny messenger among us and within us is that his or her touch is both of need *and* care. The physical child touches to receive and to give at the same time. Infant Dennis touches his mother's fingers under the door to be comforted and thereby gives comfort to an equally frightened young mother.

The duality of motivation is a powerful experience in the Christian life together. We give as we receive. We receive as we give. Such twofold ministry enables us to touch something quite deep in the persons facing need. I can accept your touch of love because I know that you are able to enjoy my touch as well.

The Starchild ability to touch body and spirit is probably one of the most important aspects of human need. Countless people wander through lonely streets, empty jobs, and friendless churches without ever being touched by another human being! Old people know that skin hungers when no one strokes, caresses, or gently squeezes the body that is aching for massage. The young person gripped in the red-hot energy of Saturday-night fever longs for the mature extensions of his or her physical birthright begun the moment those adult hands slapped air into his or her body.

The children in the congregation can lead us into the Body of Christ. They take us by the hand and lead us to the Father. There is no guile, no lust, no exotic suspicion in the ministry of these Starchildren. They suggest that such a means of celebration is open to the young and old.

PROPOSITION 6

STARCHILDREN KNOW NOTHING OF PREJUDICE.

Too Young to Know Worse

I had just led a workshop in a tiny town in rural south Australia. In conversation over a cup of coffee I asked my acquaintance if he was a local. "No," he said. "I've only been here twelve years. But I guess in another four or five years they will classify me as a local." Although he spoke with a twinkle in his eye, subsequent conversation revealed that there was truth in what he said.

The next morning was sparkling fresh. The two sons of my host, Lauchlan and Gavin, certainly did their bit to add to the liveliness of my morning. As I had plenty of time, I asked if I could walk to school with them.

They were young enough to be proud to have my company. We had only walked half a block when other children joined our party. Once names were exchanged, all kinds of information followed.

They told me about their pets, the dangers they had been through, the accidents they had survived, and even showed the battle scars. More than that they wanted me to know the stories of their town. For instance: "Did you know that Mrs. Blackburn puts her rubbish in the paddock? Well, yesterday when she bent down, a ram came up behind her and butted her over. And did you know that she is in the hospital with twelve stitches—in her head?"

Next morning I had an opportunity once again to walk to school with Lauchlan and Gavin. This time it seemed as if the other children were waiting. They greeted me like an old friend. Walking to the school surrounded by children, whom now I knew by name and who knew me by name, made me feel very much at home.

Later that day I was struck by the irony of it all. As far as the adults in that town were concerned, you had to live there sixteen years to be thought of as a local.

In the face of this my contact with the small children gave a totally different impression. I was befriended by them on the first day, and they treated me as a friend on the second day. Clearly, by the next week, I would have been fully accepted as part of their community and have belonged to their town.

Poor children, they didn't understand about the sixteen-year probation period. Mind you, they will find out about it. Their parents would see to that. I met them before they had been trained in such things. When I walked with them, they still had not outgrown the influence of their Starchild heritage. Some may say they were dangerously naïve. I prefer to say they were too young to know worse.

EXPOSITION

Children are not born prejudiced. In early childhood and the first years of life, children accept others on their merits. There is no pre-sorting and pre-appraisal according to race, creed, or color. To them it seems the most natural thing in the world to relate to others in friendship. Teachers tell how small children, black and white, handicapped and whole, newcomers and old-timers, play happily together. Later this will change. At about age eight the prejudices of the community will begin to be reflected in these same children.

They will begin to respond to the prejudices that come to them from the adult community.

Starchildren are already in God's kingdom. They reflect the attitudes and openness of God's kingdom. How arrogant and sinful we are when we take it upon ourselves to mold our children to our prejudices. Those who would live as citizens of Christ's kingdom must be remade in the mold of Godlike acceptance and openness which is the natural posture of their small children.

PROPOSITION 7

STARCHILDREN PROVIDE THE MOST ACCESSIBLE MOMENTS OF CARING.

Red Rover, Red Rover, Send Ice Cream Over

My first awareness of the caring power in children came one summer when I sold ice cream in a large city. I couldn't believe the respect and friendship acquired by merely donning my white uniform and boarding my gleaming truck with the bells.

Ice cream stirs the deepest sensuality of children. They can touch, see, and taste once again the basic memories of their earliest life in a jazzed up, nutty, chocolate-layered, crunchy form.

Mouths would water when I appeared. In the minds of these small children I became the personification of everything desirable. I wasn't just the ice-cream man. They would chant, "Ice cream, ice cream, ice cream." The children of the streets transformed me into both medium and message. I *was* ice cream.

The daily trek over the same streets provided an opportunity for great friendships. I would spend a lot of time talking with the kids on the route. One day my truck gave up the ghost. It was gleaming white on the outside, but the motor had seen better days. My limited knowledge of mechanical things wasn't much help. Despair crept over me. I knew that a delay would keep me from completing my route. My income depended on each sale.

When the kids on the street heard that the old truck

would not budge, there was an outbreak of applause. "The ice cream will be here all day." A cheer filled the air. "We will have him on our street all the time." More clapping as I looked over the twenty dirty faces smiling at me. "You can come to my house."

I thanked my friends for their hospitality. I couldn't keep back my disappointment over the broken truck. I told them that I was going to be married that summer to the girl I love. Several kids giggled. A few looked at me with wonder. I went on with my tale of woe. If I could not sell the ice cream, it would be very hard on us since we had very little money. I was almost sorry that I had told the kids my plight with so much honesty. They were quite saddened.

I slid behind the wheel and tried to make the old machine turn over. It was useless. I suddenly felt a strange rocking sensation. I stepped down from the cab, and at the back of the truck I saw twenty small children trying to push the huge vehicle. Every face showed strain as they took on this overwhelming task. They were determined to help their friend "Ice Cream."

Red Rover, Red Rover, Send Jill Over

The tension is acute. The lawn mower is hopelessly broken. At least, there is no way I can get it to work. The lawn is so high I can barely see the tips of dogs' ears as they pass through the grass. Any minute three friends from out of state will pop in for a stay. My friend from Australia has already arrived. The sewer has just backed up into the basement, and our efforts to unplug the mess just produce more sewer gas and dirty hands and feet. The phone keeps ringing with new demands for time.

As I sit at my desk shaking my head in despair, nine-year-old Jill appears with a joyous smile. She proudly offers me something to get me out of my depression. She extends an ice tray of "Coke cubes. Here is something to make you relax."

Red Rover, Red Rover, Send Amy Over

It had been so satisfying. A dream had mushroomed into a reality. Three weeks of interviewing and planning have been shaped into an exciting two-and-a-half-hour radio special on drugs. Somehow my quest had a deep personal investment. No one else seemed to sense how much this particular show had meant to me. It marked my realization of how radio could be used in a different way. The station management had been sluggish in encouraging me. The family was focused on other concerns.

I sat in my studio editing it for a repeat airing. Twelve-year-old Amy dropped in to ask for some help with her homework. I found myself pouring out my enthusiasm for the show. She watched me with patience and special sensitivity. "This show must make you feel very good." I couldn't help smiling. She was catching my feelings perfectly without understanding fully the object of my joy. This child/woman was identifying with my emotions and caring for me completely.

Red Rover, Red Rover, Send a Child Over

The man is sitting in the hospital waiting room. Tears roll down his cheeks. His shoulders rise and fall as he sobs with his head in his hands. When the grief can bring no more sobs, he moans like a foghorn wailing in the night.

The waiting-room occupants wait for visiting hours to start. People shift on the uncomfortably hard benches. They are under emotional stress. In their embarrassment over the man's suffering, they don't know what to do. Perhaps this pain is a bit too close. It may awaken the hidden fear they feel for their own loved ones.

A small child squirms loose from her mother's arms and runs around the bench. The tired woman does little to constrain the active child. The toddler plays with the ashtray, the water fountain, and the reading material. Ashes, water, and discarded magazines follow in her wake.

The twenty people in the room discover that it is easier to focus on this curious child than to deal with the sobbing old man. She finally stops in front of the suffering adult. Her face becomes intent. She moves forward carefully and looks seriously and deeply as tears roll down the face of this grief-stricken person.

The waiting room becomes silent. All eyes focus on this child-adult encounter. What will the child do to this man who should be left alone? She toddles to his knees. Her hand reaches out to his face, and she wipes the tears from his cheeks.

"All right, all right, all right," she says gently. The man opens his eyes. The shape of his mouth changes slowly. He gazes as the littlest one in the room continues to roughly wipe his face. He gently catches her hand between his wrinkled fingers and kisses it.

EXPOSITION

Caring is one of the basic gifts of the Incarnation. There is a touch of tenderness in the manger scene that prepares the way for the Christ child's coming. The women preparing the body of Jesus for death and burial highlight another caring moment in salvation history. The beginning and end are touched with care so simple and direct that it often passes unnoticed. Such simple care is what every person in the fragmented and lonely world needs and longs for.

It would seem natural that Christ's people would celebrate and relish the opportunities to be with and care for one another. The wounds to our dignity and personhood can be treated with the salve of tender care because of what Christ has suffered and given. Yet so many folk move through the church door on their trek home after the service without giving or receiving such care.

The child demands that we give and receive such basic care. The patterns of tenderness from God come tumbling back into the world as the child reaches out to others. But often faith communions without a strong agenda of caring will efficiently prevent the Starchild's making this contribution to them. A child crying out for comfort is quickly snatched from the worship service and silenced somewhere else. The young and the old are separated to study, have fellowship, worship, and serve according to age. The Body of Christ, already divided by the hate and cruelty of the world, is further drawn and quartered by age groupings in the church.

Most psychologists concede that the front lines of counseling are held by the neighbor, friend, or clergy. Yet the church community as a whole does little to support and nurture this basic ministry of caring. At this very moment many neighbors are sitting across from one another at kitchen tables. One may be telling the other through tears that she must leave her husband. Christ is in that encounter. The Starchild qualities of simple care and tenderness are called for. The distressed woman is not looking for a therapist. She wants someone to care as she charters the lonely journey she must make.

We need look only to the Starchildren to experience this gift. Caring is just a sniffle or a giggle away in the company of the child within and among us.

PROPOSITION 8

STARCHILDREN EMBODY AND ENABLE GIFTS OF THE SPIRIT.

Awakening

The students at the evening course I was teaching looked uniformly bored. Teen-agers and older folk alike all looked jaded, and nothing I did seemed to evoke the slightest response in them. I guessed that many of them had skipped the evening meal to be there and were now counting the minutes till it was all over. A young mother who was taking the course had brought her small baby with her. The baby was sleeping in a crib. I had no sooner made the point about small children and their noises being welcome in worship when the baby awoke. Immediately the little babe began to snuffle and cry softly. The mother rose from her seat and was obviously about to take her out.

It was then that it hit me: She is going to do exactly what I have been suggesting should not be done. I asked her to please not take the baby out. She was reluctant to comply. The baby continued to cry. In the grip of a wild impulse, I walked to the back of the class, leaned down over the crib, and picked the baby up. With every eye upon me and my own heart beating much faster than normal, I carried the babe to the front of the class. I had not the faintest idea what I was going to do next. To my utter amazement, the baby stopped crying. But something even more amazing was in store.

I looked up from the baby to the audience. That group of tired, bored, and unresponsive people was gone. In their place was an audience both alert and animated. Smiles beamed from every face. As I looked at them, I realized this magical transformation had been worked by a tiny baby. This infant had unknowingly touched every life with gentleness and brought joy to every face.

I pointed out to the congregation what had happened and asked why they were smiling. They couldn't answer me. They knew they felt good. They knew they felt tender. But they didn't know why. We noted another strange thing. Even people who were quite unable to see the babe's face were equally touched with joy just at the sight of my holding her.

EXPOSITION

In my head I had come to recognize that children are an important part of the Body of Christ. I boldly proclaimed that, as such, children should be accepted and welcomed in the worshiping community. What's more, I asserted that their presence would add something to that assembly. That is, just as with other members of the Body, babies would have something of value to contribute. Luckily for me, when I first began to say this no one asked me what this contribution would be. I didn't have any idea. All I knew was that they must bring something.

On one thing I was clear. The murmurings and whimperings of a human baby are not offensive sounds, not even in the house of God. Therefore, such natural noises should by themselves be no reason for withdrawing a baby from a service of worship.

In recent years I have become increasingly interested in symbols. I have discovered old symbols and invented new ones. I have had groups examine symbols, find meaning in symbols, and pray with symbols. As I looked at that group and wondered why they had suddenly come alive, I wondered if it was because the baby was a symbol. Could it be that I was holding in my arms the most powerful symbol of hope in the universe? Whatever it was, that baby had power to evoke tenderness and joy. Furthermore, the baby had accomplished this with a group that was very diverse in age and interest.

Tenderness and joy are fruits of the spirit. These were gifts I constantly tried to nourish in my congregation—often without success. Could it be that these were the gifts that our babies can bring to us if the other members of the Body are open to receive them?

PROPOSITION 9

EVERY OLD PERSON CARRIES A STARCHILD LOCKED INSIDE.

Starchild, Starchild, Come Out and Play

It was my first visit to the Deep South since my civil rights days. The Southern Baptists were my hosts for the Mississippi and Alabama teaching tour. A minister with sporty black and white wing-tip shoes and white suit introduced me to the thirty adults. They were church members interested in the teaching ministry.

I don't know what I had expected to find in rural Alabama. These farm folk actually had red necks! The sun broiled their exposed skin to a lobster red. Their necks and arms glowed in the church basement.

They had asked me to focus on creative ways to teach the Bible. After calling them into small groups, I gave each the passage from Genesis 1 and told them to plan a learning experience without using language to communicate with one another. They went about their task with relish and enthusiasm.

When we shared a few minutes later, I was delighted by the creativity of these farm folk. After the groups had led us through what they had designed in silence, I asked if there were anything else to be shared.

An old man with bib overalls raised his hand. He was in his sixties. His face and hands were wrinkled like a freshly plowed field. He walked into the center of our circle. The old Southern Baptist moved into a crouched position and began performing a dance of creation! His hands and body beautifully reflected the struggle for birth and growth. It was a stunning experience to see the guileless dance of a child emerge from this old, conservative body. I glanced around the room. There were tears in the eyes of many. He was carrying all of us back into the act of creation with his unrehearsed dance of life. His grandchildren had freed him for a dance that he alone knew.

It had been a bad summer. Probably the most demanding test of our lives. The liberating environment of Chicago was gone after seven years. We were now buried in south-western Pennsylvania at a small Christian college. The school was on the rocks, financially and academically. A grant from a foundation had created the job I held. It was my task to stimulate intellectual and spiritual ferment. In spite of my short haircut and tie, it had been an uphill battle to find support from the establishment for my struggle to awaken students and faculty.

When the students had scattered for the summer and faculty friends had undertaken their journeys of research and rest, my boss called me to his office and fired me. I had worked too closely with the black students. Suddenly no one in the town would speak to us. The remaining faculty members would look the other way when we entered the grocery store.

One day I was stopped in the library by the frail old woman who always seemed buried in library work. She said, "Would you and your wife come for dinner today?"

I was surprised that she spoke to me. Her invitation sounded too good to be true. Marilyn and I didn't know what to expect when we knocked at her door. In the course of the evening we discovered one of the truly radical persons in the town. She read all the underground papers and had strong feelings concerning injustice and war. Her secret life included many hours of caring for small children. Their spirit filled her. This old woman was much younger in her idealism and beliefs than any of the students I had met during my stay at the college. She not only knew about the issues of the day but how things had to be changed.

This hippie was old and gray. Her body showed the wear of years. Yet she was a Starchild breaking into a new world of hope and service. By day she was the mild-mannered librarian, but at a moment's notice she was ready to pop into her sneakers and become a child again.

Her eyes sparkled. It seemed that she would spring from her seat at any moment. She had been through a serious heart operation and several other extremely threatening health conditions in the past few years. Yet she always seemed on the edge of exploding with excitement.

She and her husband were special friends. They were the pastoral team that welcomed a college student to his first parish work. They loved the new youth minister and thrust him into all kinds of growing experiences. They seemed ancient then and still do twenty-three years later. Yet they are the youngest ministerial folk I have ever met.

She always has dozens of very young piano students. Mrs. Howey always rides the swell of their words. She seems to bubble with the enthusiasm they feel when they play the first tune. She is the child broken free to embrace all of life and all of those in it.

This wrinkled couple seems to have never lost the wrinkled babe within.

EXPOSITION

Eric Berne and the host of folk who followed the master of Transactional Analysis have provided us with some convenient handles for looking at the different dimensions of our personhood. The child, parent, and adult in each of us vie for control. We deal with these "tapes" in differing ways.

It seems to us that the child is one of the most difficult aspects of our personhood. At least, the society conditions us to repress this source of play, imagination, and creativity. Only when we run the adult and parent tapes do we experience the most complete rewards from the systems through which we move.

One of the real gifts of growing old is that we are permitted to free the child within us. As elders of the tribe, we are released to be more complete. Maggie Kuhn, the founder of the Gray Panthers, and others have reminded us that many old people are conditioned to play only a parent role. They are unable to live in the fullness of their personhood because they have been in the captivity of social systems for too long.

By segregating the young and old, the middle-aged easily maintain oppressive systems. Both the young and the old can be treated as if they were "childish." Maggie Kuhn calls the patronizing programs for the aged "glorified playpens for wrinkled babies." Anything stressing our service *for* others implies our condescension toward them.

Old people who are in touch with the Starchild qualities *are* related to children. But they *are not* childish. We are suggesting that liberated old people in the local congregation may offer one of the best opportunites for the qualities of Starchildren to be released within your faith family. It may be that such old people are one real hope for the future of our society. These living archives are the personification of our history and roots. They may become the cutting, revolutionary edge of a more faithful future.

The very young and the very old belong together.

PROPOSITION 10

STARCHILDREN ARE THE
ONLY GUIDES TO THE KINGDOM.

Testimony

A friend drew to my attention a position being advertised by the Australian Council of Churches Education. The way the job was described, it seemed likely that it could be the kind of part-time job I was looking for. However, I was not enthusiastic. The problem was that the job required spending a whole year looking at children in the church. For me this was old turf, turf I wanted to leave behind. I had undertaken church research studies in the past. However, time and circumstance closed in on me, and expediency dictated I should apply. Eventually, I was appointed to the position.

What I expected happened. As news filtered out that I had taken the job, the comments began to flow. Some of my friends thought it amusing that I had chosen to spend a whole year thinking about children. Others quite boldly suggested it was a backward step. I got the message and generally shared this latter point of view. The way I sought to hang onto my respectability was to make it as plain as I could that this "children's thing" was a short-term venture. When I was with other ministers, I was careful to explain that "as soon as this assignment is over, I will be quickly into more *significant* ministries."

As I got into the job, some quite unexpected dynamics

began to move me about. The first thing I became aware of was that this whole subject of children was of critical importance to the contemporary church.

Against a background of declining membership, the conviction grew in me that ministering with children was a key issue. That is, what congregations had been doing or not doing for their children, to their children, and with their children had been an important contributing factor in this recent malaise. What is more, the way we related to our children in the now and in the future would have a decisive influence for either growth or decline. Now this was a fairly wild thought. It was generally presumed that the church influenced its children. I was beginning to think it could be the other way around.

Other questions continued to gnaw at me. I was never really happy with such statements as "The children of today are the church of tomorrow." Certainly, I could see the truth in this statement. But I suspected there was much more at stake than this. The question was, What?

The anthropologist Margaret Mead was a key person in helping me focus on just what else was at stake. In her writings she suggests that babies, toddlers, and children have an essential role to play in keeping a community vigorous and viable—the point being that babies, toddlers, and children somehow revitalize the communities that value them. The reverse side of this is that any community that does not care for its children cuts itself off from a primary source of life and consequently is in grave danger. This danger is not just that the children will suffer through lack of care. It is entirely likely that the community deprived of the life-giving juices that children supply will totally collapse. I began to wonder if this could be what was wrong with many of the disheartened congregations that had long since forsaken their active ministry with children.

These thoughts set others rolling. I began to wonder if

Jesus was saying something similar to this when he said of children that "of such is the kingdom of heaven." Thoughts began to boom within me like distant thunder. I searched out everything Jesus said about children.

Two things are clear. One is that it is a very serious thing to do anything that will hinder a child's accepting God's love. The second is that those who would live in God's kingdom must be willing to learn from children. According to Jesus, small children are of the Kingdom in a unique way.

A new thought formed within me, and this began to shake my previous assumptions. I had always presumed that children, and especially small children, knew nothing about God. On the other hand, because of my experience, my years, my theological training, etc., I thought that I knew lots about God. Therefore, it followed that the situation was this: If I didn't tell children what I knew about God, the little varmints would miss out on God's love and not enter his Kingdom. Now my new thought was pushing me in quite a different direction. Could it be that Jesus was saying that if I didn't learn from children that I would miss out on his Kingdom?

EXPOSITION

Looking back over my experience with children in the church, I have to admit that I had spent lots of time patting children on the head. For the first time, I began to realize that Jesus was asking me to look them in the eyes. I came to understand that, for me, this looking children in the eyes was no optional extra. For the sake of my own spiritual growth it was essential.

I think I know now something of what Jesus meant when he talked about the necessity of being converted and becoming like a little child. For me it means being with babies, toddlers, and children in quite a new way. It means being open to receive the gospel of healing and wholeness as it comes to me through them. Certainly, I am well aware that I have gifts of knowledge and insight to share with them. As they grow, they will need me to tell them the stories of the Bible and of their friend and Savior Jesus. On my part, I will continue to learn new things about him as I experience his Spirit in them.

PROPOSITION 11

STARCHILDREN ARE GOD'S DOCTORS.

Friendly Skies

At the best of times flying tends to be boring. When you have had to rise three hours before normal and skip breakfast in the bargain, it is positively dreary. They called this the "early-bird intercapital businessmen's flight," and it certainly lived up to its name. It was all gray suits and briefcases. Leaning back and trying to catch a few winks of sleep, snatches of conversations about mergers, quotas, and sales projections floated my way.

When I opened my eyes, I could hardly believe them. She was laughing. Not just a practiced smile with her lips. Even her eyes were laughing. I did not remember ever seeing an airline hostess laugh. Well, at least not like that. Naturally, I wanted to be in on the joke. But, to my frustration, I couldn't see even though I should have been able to from my aisle seat. The problem was that everyone else was looking too. My view was obscured by business suits and business heads, bald and hairy (but all well-groomed, of course). Everyone with an aisle seat was leaning into the aisle. And to add to my curiosity, I could hear laughter filtering down from the front seats. I just had to know what was causing this pre-breakfast merriment. Whatever it was, it had to be good.

And it was. A little boy, I suspect not yet three, had been given the freedom of the aisle. Moving from seat to seat, he was giving every row the biggest smiles. When he reached my seat, he grasped the arm and said, "Ah, boo!" He turned me on. He had done the same thing for the whole airplane. Wherever I looked, I could see executives, sales managers, and computer programmers smiling broadly.

I've flown on airlines when, in an effort to mitigate the boredom, airline attendants appear in new ensembles every hour of flight. If the passengers appreciated this unique service, they certainly kept their appreciation to themselves. Yet one small boy transmitted smiles and laughter the length of a whole aircraft. I am not sure what he had; but whatever it was, it stroked and tickled everyone aboard.

He only walked the aisle for a few minutes. Nonetheless, even after he was seated again with his mother, the smiles lingered on. The atmosphere in the cabin was relaxed. The early-bird flight was flying in friendly skies.

EXPOSITION

There are polite laughs and belly laughs, put-on laughs and put-off laughs. There are some smiles that are cosmetic and superficial. There are some smiles that well up from within and burst out because there is no way they can be held back.

Babies and toddlers evoke such welling-up-from-within smiles. They do it for all ages and can do it in all circumstances. Most times they have no knowledge that they are doing it. Their ability to make us smile is neither contrived nor practiced. What is it about them that makes us smile so deeply?

Is it not that they are just themselves? so glad to be alive? so pleased to be with us? willing to befriend total strangers? ready to flash radiant smiles at anyone who will reciprocate?

No matter how gloom has taken hold of a person's spirit,

the smile and laughter of a child can penetrate its darkness. Through their smiles and laughter, the babies and toddlers keep passing on messages of hope. These messages go something like this. "I'm OK and you're OK, and it is great to be together!" These messages come without qualifications and are transmitted with total enthusiasm.

Laughter is the medicine of the soul. Our Starchildren are God-given doctors of the spirit.

PROPOSITION 12

STARCHILDREN DIE FOR OUR SINS.

Falling Food Sticks

Dennis had urged and cajoled us to take to the streets of Pittsburgh. Armed with cassette recorders, we went in search of people. Our aim was to hear them tell their stories.

In a downtown fast-food restaurant, two boys caught our attention. Their faces told us they were preteen. Their dress and their cigarettes were calculated to give the impression that they were older. They were offhanded when we asked if we could sit at their table. However, there was quite a ripple of interest when we asked if we could interview them. Over the next hour we listened to their stories. We began to understand why these two boys wanted to give the impression that they were tough young men.

In a way they were tough. Certainly they both bore the scars of life's onslaughts. Both were from broken homes. Both were facing painful and confusing family readjustments. Both now had money in their pockets, but neither of them was happy with his life situation.

We asked them if they had any idea why their parents had broken up. Their response was to stare at the table. Finally, one boy looked up. "Well, we gave Mom a helluva time." He explained that his mother had been so badly treated that she had no option other than to leave. We inquired as to who in particular had ill-treated his mother. There were more stares at the table. "Well, we kids did." We could not hide our surprise. The boy looked shamefaced. "We did lots of very bad things. For a start, I used to swear a lot and—" We waited, feeling his pain. "And my little four-year-old brother, well—he even used to throw his food on the floor." His eyes reddened, and once again he stared down at the table. The message was clear. This boy was sure that his bad language and his brother's bad manners had broken up his parents' marriage. We listened while his friend gave us another variation on this same theme.

No wonder they were trying their best to look tough. How could they ever let anyone know that within them their hearts were bleeding? These boys were living with the belief that they had caused their parents to separate. There is little to smile about when you're so burdened with guilt. And only God knows just how that little four-year-old was feeling.

EXPOSITION

At times we speak of the heavy load of responsibility children place upon adults. Generally, there is less attention given to the way adults can, and frequently do, burden children with loads for which they can have no possible responsibility.

Children are sensitive to every nuance and mood of the significant adults who surround them. What is more, they have a sense that the mood of the environment is somewhat dependent on them. They hear angry voices and quickly jump to the conclusion that somehow the anger is directed toward them. They feel hostility in the air and suppose that they are the cause. This characteristic makes them extremely vulnerable to exploitation.

Adults who are unwilling or unable to accept responsibility for their own problems look around for someone else to blame. For many who live with children, the solution is all too easy. "Obviously, the kids are to blame." Frequently, those who take this route are aware that this is far from the real truth. But for the adult, it is a way of coping; and besides, the children seem so ready to take the blame for just about everything.

So it is that children suffer alongside their significant adults. Many times it is far more than suffering *with* them; the children are suffering *for* them. Perhaps this is at the root of the Old Testament concept of the sins of the fathers being visited upon the children. It seems that mothers could also be included in this. How many Starchildren have been crushed as they have taken upon themselves the heavy emotional loads of the adults who are important to them?

PROPOSITION 13

JESUS IS A STARCHILD.

Up, Jesus, Up

Murray had the curiosity and excitement of a toddling child. His whole world came alive with every encounter. My seminary roommate could not take even the simplest campus walk without stumbling upon a world alive with mystery, humor, and adventure. He might discover a man with a talking chicken in front of the bar across from the seminary on his way to get a newspaper.

He would sweep into our room and sit on my desk to tell me his latest discovery. His wild descriptions were always accompanied by wild gestures with his arms. These thrashing windmills always seemed to hit my small wood carving of Jesus that a friend had brought back from Poland. The poor head would break off and roll under the chair. Without slowing the pace of his story, Murray would open my desk drawer and use the glue there to replace the head of Jesus. With a certain appreciation for his own craftsmanship, Murray would replace the carving on the shelf saying, "Up, Jesus, up."

There was a star. It was a strange star. Men wise and learned saw it. So did many others. It was clear to all that the star announced a special child. The mother holding the babe in her arms knew also. This tiny one would go many miles, do many things for many people before he would rest. They all came to worship this small King of kings. He is our Starchild.

Anna speaks slowly: "Deanna is a mongoloid. My daughter is now in her teens. Yet she is a child. It has been a wondrous experience being parents who grow older while our child stays young. However, it makes us remain young too.

"There is something special about such a child, or woman. She elicits unusual responses in others. She seems to bring out God qualities in others. She loves baptism. She will often move through the house with her cross. 'In the name of the Father, Son, and Holy Spirit.' "

He was stunned by the news tearfully delivered. His friend was dead. The mourning of the family was severe. Jesus wept.

EXPOSITION

The most stunning aspect of following Jesus Christ is that he seems to reveal different facets of his personhood to different people. So many different layers of his character and nature become clear in the lives of his followers. Serious students of the Bible find more and more as they dig deeper and deeper. He walks with the pacifist. Soldiers also feel his companionship and support. The rich know him personally; so do the wretched and poor. Saint and sinner can claim his fellowship. Liberals and conservatives are both close to their Lord.

There are not many different Jesus persons. However, he does meet each person in his or her context and understanding. Yet no one completely captures him in his or her mind and spirit. Jesus is always a bit more complex.

He belongs to all; and yet he loves you and me especially.

In our weakness and fear, we long to have Jesus clearly defined and limited. We want a God who fits our limited spiritual realm. We stop being children of wonder and awe as we grow older. The expanding Christ is no longer welcome.

The Starchild finds great comfort in running, skipping, and sleeping in the companionship of Jesus. He is a friend and lover.

There are special Starchild qualities available through Jesus. He is past, present, and future. He is completely human with the senses attuned to his world. Yet he is also completely God and therefore beckons us to go beyond our past understandings.

Jesus lived the qualities of forgiveness, sacrifice, and righteousness. The words of his mouth and the deed of his life were one and the same.

We want to put Jesus on a shelf. It is easy to remove our lives from him. Starchildren enable us to get in touch with the Jesus waiting to reveal himself more and more completely to us. As we love the smallest of those in our midst, so we touch Jesus and are touched by him.

PROPOSITION 14

THOSE WHO REJECT STARCHILDREN
REJECT LIFE.

Moonrise

Barry has taken the long journey through depression to nervous breakdown and back. His son, Andrew, had lots to do with his climb back to health. The role played by Andrew in his father's recovery was something very few people expected.

In previous days Andrew had contributed greatly to Barry's breakdown. Although Andrew has the body of a fifteen-year-old, his mind stopped growing at four. Barry never could get used to the fact that Andrew would not progress beyond that point. As Barry watched neighbors' children learning new skills and maturing, Andrew seemed to become more childish and less able to cope. Barry's disappointment in Andrew grew and compounded till resentment ravaged Barry's mind and spirit.

Gradually, Barry's therapist enabled him to see that his rejection of Andrew had been a cause of his breakdown. With the help of his counselor, Barry began to see Andrew in a new light. He was enabled to see Andrew as he was and not just as he had determined he should be. Viewed from this new perspective, Barry found the real Andrew to be more attractive than he had ever dreamed possible. This change in Barry set off a reaction in Andrew. Very tentatively Andrew began to explore new ways of relating to his father.

At Andrew's Sunday school, one of his teachers had made a connection between the rising of the sun and moon and the constantly renewed love of God. Andrew became totally enthralled by this concept. He asked his father if he would sit with him and watch the moonrise.

On the night of full moon, the whole family sat on the porch facing the eastern horizon. As the moon climbed over the edge of the mountains, Andrew shook with excitement. Then as it moved into full view, he did something he had never done before. Andrew reached out and encircled his father in his arms. Barry was completely taken by surprise. Tears streamed down his face. Andrew continued to grip his father. He spoke in awed tones. "I've never seen the moonrise before. Have you, Dad?" Barry was too caught up in his emotions to manage a reply.

A few more minutes passed in silence. It was as if Andrew's awe was infectious. It was as if none of them had ever seen the moonrise before. When the moon was fully launched into the night sky, Andrew announced, "God keeps loving all of us, you know, Dad."

Every month now, Andrew and his family wait together on their porch to watch the moonrise. Andrew and Barry always sit with their arms around each other.

EXPOSITION

Handicapped children require much of their parents. They usually must have special care. Their needs frequently determine the shape of large areas of family life. In one way or another, they make their presence felt in all the family's social relationships, on every vacation, and even in their parents' bedroom.

It is not at all uncommon for whole communities to reject their obviously handicapped children. Special funds may be allocated to them, but these are usually utilized to ensure that these persons have a life of their own, on their own, away from the rest of the community.

The parents of handicapped children frequently share community attitudes and quite naturally are influenced by its prejudices. When the community measures health and wholeness in terms of physical prowess and IQ ratings, the parent of the handicapped can feel cheated. It is understandable that these parents should feel that life has been unfair. Such thoughts often lead to inner resentment.

There is another side to all this. Handicapped children do not just require special attention, they are both willing and able to give special attention. However, as with all giving, it can only be experienced by those who are aware that it is being offered and who are willing to receive it. The gifts the handicapped have to offer can be easily overlooked. In fact, they will never even be noticed by communities and individuals who view the handicapped simply as things to be cared for. Only those who recognize them as persons to be loved and valued will ever perceive their gifts. They will enable the handicapped to give out of their own special richness. Then it will be seen that though they may be deficient in some ways, they are not short on love and affirmation and loyalty.

It is sometimes said that we are all crippled. Our handicaps may not be obvious, but they are reflected in our fractured relationships, our neuroses, and our addictions. God sends his Starchildren to challenge us, to revitalize us, to heal us, and to make us whole. To reject and resent them is to turn our back on the source of life. To resent them is to increase enormously the dreadful possibility that we will die in our resentments and neuroses.

PROPOSITION 15

TO BE BORN AGAIN IS TO BECOME A STARCHILD.

Unto Us Is Born a Starchild

The comedian had responded very strongly to me. Our friendly conversation had been the opening bridge to a much deeper sharing. We walked from the television studio where we had been interviewed. He took me to a small restaurant off Broadway. The place was noisy and busy. I strained to absorb his intense conversation.

It had been a hard road for him. His initial success had come swiftly. The fact that he did the most popular imitation of John F. Kennedy made his records an instant success. He had $500,000 on hand when the Dallas tragedy ended his act. No one wanted a comedy routine about the fallen president.

The comedian's world was swept away. He turned to drugs and liquor to deal with his loss of fame. It went from bad to worse for him. The eight years that followed were empty and cruel. His health started to fail.

He stopped his story and smiled broadly. "I have found Jesus!" Vaughn launched into the amazing story of his rebirth. As he pushed on with his testimony, he kept referring to his grandmother's influence. "She raised me. She took me to church every Sunday. She really gave me a good foundation."

He had been born again. The human wreck was now a

vibrant, believing person. He had not climbed back into his mother's womb. However, he was now in touch with his Starchild past.

Pastors have gathered from miles around. It is a rare opportunity to share creative ideas for isolated ministries. Suddenly, a young man in his twenties can't suppress his need to talk. "I was a sinner." This is the third time we have heard the story. Each time he recounts his loss of innocence, tears fill his eyes.

At the break, I approach Les and ask if he will share his story on tape for me. He eagerly tells the tale of wandering from God into a far country of sin.

As I watch him talk, I am not sure if he is mentally ill or just in the grip of a spiritual awakening. I do know that I like him and respect his desperate quest.

As I pack my belongings for the trip home, Les approaches me shyly. "I want you to take this." He hands me two dollars.

"It is God's money. It is all that I have. Take it for your ministry."

There is a true innocence in him now. "When you came in here, I thought you were the devil. Now I know that you are my brother."

"Can I give you a love gift?" I take the cross from my neck and put it around his neck. We hug. There are tears in our eyes.

He has been born again. He is becoming a child again.

EXPOSITION

The White House, the times, and the spirit of God have made the born-again Christian media news. There is a new social acceptance of this deep and important religious act.

Radicals, criminals, and stars are stepping forward with testimonials about their rebirth. Yet there is not much evidence that the times are better or more Christ-like because of the media attention. Most folk are as confused about adults becoming babes again as was Nicodemus. He could not understand how a grown person could get back into his mother's womb. The survivors in the trenches of our culture also puzzle over how the childlike qualities lived and taught by Jesus can come to those weary and conditioned by modern adult life.

There is a strange ability by which the converted people I know become childlike. They seem to have the capacity to recycle their earlier positive experiences into strengths for the present. It is often hard for friends and family to appreciate this sudden childlike exuberance.

Enthusiasm, joy, and hope are human states often resented by those caught in the pinch between the powers and principalities that oppress them. Going back to the freshness of the birth perspective radically changes our view of life. Cynicism and enslavement are replaced by an awareness of the Kingdom.

The freshness at conversion is not unusual among children. Jesus was kind in pointing to the tiniest among us as models for the rest of us to understand the Kingdom. We are suggesting that the path to rebirth within the life of the congregation passes through those children who are not merely herded around the controlled world of adult religion.

Theology rolling back to us from the Third World suggests that our salvation may rest with the gospel as it is revealed among those who suffer and who are oppressed. The rich and comfortable may not be able to hear the Good News. Our salvation has always come through the suffering servants (Isaiah 53). This thesis may be pushed further by adding that the smallest, youngest, and least powerful in our midst are the vehicles of our rebirth. These gifts of God are with us in order to serve and give. Their ministry is a freely given gift to the whole body of the church.

The Western world has been tempted to close its eyes to the needy and hungry of the world. We have also failed to have eyes to see and ears to hear in the presence of our Starchildren. The gospel of rebirth can best be experienced by accepting the ministry of those fresh from the womb.

PROPOSITION 16

STARCHILDREN LOVE FAST.

Love Note

My stay with five-year-old Stephen and his family was only overnight. My visit would include one evening meal, breakfast, and a late-night call to collect my luggage. So we only had one night in which to get to know one another. Nonetheless, we covered a lot of ground.

Stephen showed me the hens, the dog, and his pet lizard, or more correctly, where his pet lizard used to live. He had escaped that day. In addition to his interest in living things, Stephen was also a collector of inanimate things. In the laundry room he showed me his latest acquisitions. He had assembled a fine collection of small stones, feathers, and a variety of other interesting objects. When I asked him why he had collected those particular things, he replied that he had chosen the articles "because they were useful." He explained how with the feathers he could make Indian hats and with the stones he could make patterns and houses and hundreds of other things.

After the evening meal, Stephen called, "Good night," and went off down the hall toward his bedroom. He had almost reached his destination when he turned around and came back into the living room where I was sitting alone. He walked over to my chair and kissed me. Before I could gather my wits he was gone. The softness of his kiss lingered on.

The next morning it was time for good-byes. I had been thinking about Stephen's collection. Summoning up all my boldness, I asked if I could borrow it for use in my workshops. "Why, sure," he said. Without hesitation he handed over his collection. He was obviously pleased that I had recognized its usefulness.

Since I was running late I left my things scattered over the bedroom in disarray. As I went down the path I could hear Stephen's mother telling him not to go into my bedroom.

It was 11 P.M. when I returned to the house to pick up my things. I flung everything into the cases and was quickly on my way.

It was the next day when I was in preparation for a workshop that I came across Stephen's handiwork. The day before I had left a Manila file on the bed. Sometime during the day, Stephen must have entered my room. There on the cover of the file was scrawled one word, *Stephen*. He had risked his mother's wrath in order to make his mark on my book.

That one word was like a love letter. I have a feeling that's just what Stephen intended it to be.

EXPOSITION

Sooner or later most of us come to realize that loving and hurting often go together. To love another makes one vulnerable to pain. To reach out in tenderness and warmth is to risk rejection. Why not be a rock? Why not keep people at arm's length and walk on the safe side? Surely only fools would wear their hearts on their sleeve in a world like ours. So it is that for many being cool, standing apart even when this means standing in the cold, is preferrable to the risks included in reaching toward the warmth.

Our small children behave in quite different ways. We

might do well to ask what this foreign spirit is that grips our children. Why is it that little boys want to kiss grown men whom they have only just met? Where does this reckless spirit come from? It comes from God himself. Our small children reveal God's heart. It is this species of love that led Jesus to the cross. All unknowing, our small children are moved by this same love.

PROPOSITION 17

STARCHILDREN ARE CHRISTOPHERS (BEARERS OF CHRIST).

Christopher, Christopher, Christopher

The grieving wife is struggling to overcome the fresh swell of pain as she sits with her pastor. Her husband's body has just been taken from the house. It is still so unreal, unfamiliar, unfair. Yet she has outwardly expressed no emotion.

The pastor knows that she must deal with this grief. He sits and talks with her. Something has to happen to enable this woman to put her sorrow in touch with her resources.

A small neighborhood child rushes into the room. He has not bothered to knock. This is familiar turf for him. He often dropped by to talk with the deceased. Tommy slips up on the couch next to the new widow. He casually cuddles close to her. Her arm drops down around the young child. After being silent for a couple of minutes, the five-year-old looks up at her. "It is a shame about Stephen. He was a good man. I will miss him."

The widow hugs him, and the tears roll down her cheeks as the emotional dam breaks.

The congregation worships in a special way this morning. The mission committee is delighted. The focus is an issue close to their hearts: world hunger.

After presenting a well-reasoned biblical message on this

enormous problem and the Christian's responsibility to do something about it, the worshipers are divided into discussion groups. Each cluster is asked to develop some solutions to the problem.

The expectations for creative ideas are high. This influential and intellectual parish will surely perceive what can be done to help the hungry of the world.

The sharing lives up to the expectations. The ideas for programs and fund-raising are excellent. At the end of the process, a small boy raises his hand. The pastor invites him to speak. He speaks quietly but with conviction. "If so many people in the world are hungry, why do we have so many big dogs?"

The radio talk-show host knows immediately that the caller is young, very young. He must proceed carefully.

"How old are you?"

"I am nine."

"What's on your mind?"

"Well, it is about my dad. We were out driving yesterday. We were going down this street when a dog came running out in front of us. Dad tried to stop. However, we hit him. It was a black and white puppy. Dad just kept on driving. I told him that we should stop. Maybe he wasn't killed. Just hurt. He would be suffering. We should do something. Dad didn't want to get involved. He was afraid the owner might be around."

"How do you feel about this?"

"I feel that we should have stopped. He might be suffering. It would have been the right thing to do."

The chaplain and the young doctor stand by a small hospital crib. She is hard at work. The child is connected to a variety of tubes. The chaplain knows that the situation is critical. The doctor slowly pumps a small bag with a steady rhythm. "If I stop squeezing this bag, she will be dead. I am the only thing that is keeping her alive."

The chaplain has known Joyce for the past six months. She has always seemed remote and tight. It is strange that a person with such a personality would work in a children's hospital. Joyce does not want to let any part of her emotions touch her patients.

She has also been quite critical of religion. There had been a few times when she gave the young chaplain a hard time. She could not understand how religion had anything to do with a medical facility. "The doctors do the healing. Everyone else is in the way."

However, today Joyce seems quite willing to have the chaplain for company. It has been two hours since the child became dependent on Joyce's hand for her breath.

The child's feeble fight for life has somehow removed the wall between these two adults. Their talk becomes deep and compelling.

"Am I God? Why do I have to decide whether to keep squeezing or just let her die? No one should be in this position. I am not a healer. I have been so phony. Look at that little dear. She is dead already. I am only delaying the obvious. I just can't give up on her. Why isn't God loving now? She really—I really need him now."

EXPOSITION

Every believer is called to bear the cross of Christ. The ministry of caring, teaching, celebrating, and reaching out to others belongs to the priesthood of every disciple. Yet we have often looked to the most experienced, best educated, or most saintly for such work in the faith community. The authors are proposing the utilization and the ministry of the youngest as part of the church's renewal. The gifts of honesty and innocence that so easily become dulled in adults are still accessible for the youngest. These Starchild qualities are promised to every Christian through the baptism of the faith. Yet maturation erodes and challenges the fruits of the Spirit in us.

The quest to be faithful must always be just that—a quest. We never have it made. There is always more of the journey to travel in our odyssey of faith. At each point in our trek God provides means of grace.

For our time our Christophers are the Starchildren. They have been sent that we might know new life and new faith. It is up to us to meet them and permit them to minister to us.

PROPOSITION 18

STARCHILDREN ARE COURAGEOUS.

Push, Relax, Push, Relax

It is unnerving to be hospitalized. At least, a man feels stripped when he's reduced to a short nightshirt and a bed. It is hard to become a dependent child again.

The swift flow of events leading to my admittance to a contagious-disease hospital in Detroit left me dazed. A mere "headache and back pains" drove me from my summer job in Ann Arbor to my hospital room. Friends found a very sick seminary student. They rushed me to my home in Detroit. The doctor actually visited the house and ordered me to the hospital. The building looked like one might catch a contagious disease just driving past it.

The spinal tap was painful. They insisted that I remain flat on my back. The table reminded me of the morgue slabs depicted in those cheap cop movies. I remained alone on the examining-room table for hours. I hurt and I was scared. How could God do this to such a nice guy! Why me, Lord? These were the kind of self-pitying thoughts that drifted through my mind.

The weeks in the polio ward were filled with more discouragement and pain. People just didn't get polio in 1959. But I had. The therapist was determined to bring me out of my despair and self-pity. She was also committed to make my body do things it had never been able to do before my hospitalization.

Between those sessions of hot compresses and twisting,

she applied the most important aspect of her healing art. She would bring in a small baby who had contracted a much more severe case of polio than I. Placing the child on my bed, she would start her work with the tiny child. "See how the baby works to resist the pressure of my hand. He is a very courageous person. Andy will cooperate with all my therapy. You would think he knows that I am twisting and pulling to make him better. He never cries and fusses. It hurts him, you know. It has to hurt in order for him to improve. However, I don't think that I can ever get him back to where a normal child would be. Very courageous little fellow." She was letting this child make me better.

Andrea also helped me improve. She was older than Andy. She must have been three or four years old. She had her braces. My therapist friend had been able to make her understand that when she could walk the length of the hall on her own, she could go home.

Several times a day I watched this small girl struggling up the hall. My room had a huge observation window in it. The child looked so strange—a small body with its huge silver braces. She wore a helmet to protect herself against the many falls she took.

A nurse or the therapist would take her hands as she battled to guide her weak legs. Beads of sweat stood out on her forehead. Her undershirt would be wet after a few minutes of hall work.

After days of walking she ventured with less support from helping hands. I shuddered as she tumbled to the floor. Tears came to her eyes, but she did not cry. Andrea merely bit her lip and started once again.

My therapist would stand at the door as we both watched the child struggle. "She is really something, isn't she?" I could only nod. I could see in the professional's face the deep appreciation that was often masked by her toughness in dealing with us.

I knew what this dedicated woman was doing with me. She was permitting two children to heal me. Andy and Andrea made me whole again.

EXPOSITION

Courage is not a very popular religious or cultural attribute these days. Folk in the Western world are very much into their own personal concerns. Sex, religion, politics, and drugs are all individual interests in many circles. Perhaps it is the uncertainty of the times that tempts people into this kind of inner life. Inflation, lack of security, corruption, and meaninglessness seem to infect the young and old in dramatic ways.

The Starchild has a special mission in such times. The witness of courage is most clearly manifested among the very young. It is sometimes hard for the adult to perceive such profiles in courage. How can we look to a child for courage when he or she is afraid of the dark or a spider? Yet when we put on the spectacles of Jesus, we see what courage the tiniest can show us.

It is an extreme act of courage to leap into deep water when swimming is new and frightening. It is a courageous act to pilot that two-wheeler for the first time when there are no parental hands safely holding it.

The courage sparkling in the lives of our Starchildren is there for us to rediscover and imitate.

PROPOSITION 19

STARCHILDREN ARE APOSTLES
OF COMMUNITY.

Offers That Could Not Be Refused

Murray is a New Zealand Christian educator whose life has been touched by children. He now sees it as part of his work to help congregations let their children touch them.

Murray was invited by a congregation he had not previously visited to lead a Sunday worship service on the theme of Christian fellowship. As a lead-in to this subject he decided he would ask the children to join him for a few minutes at the front of the church.

Prior to the service he was taken aside and quietly told that this congregation was not used to doing "unusual things." Apparently Murray's reputation had preceded him. When he looked out over the congregation they certainly seemed very straight and stiff. For a moment his courage wavered; but seeing children dotted here and there, Murray decided to risk it.

When Murray asked the children to come forward, they hesitated. Murray stood waiting, smiling directly at the children who were within his view. Then in ones and twos they came. There gathered around him ten small children.

Murray talked with them. He told them that the church was like a big family made up of people of all sizes and shapes and all the stages and ages of life. Murray explained that all of those different kinds of people were needed if the

Christian family was to be complete. He asked the children to help him illustrate the inclusive nature of the Christian family. They readily agreed. Murray asked the children to go into the congregation and to bring back one other person. The goal of this exercise was to bring together at the front of the church a representative group of all the different people who were worshiping together that morning.

The ten children made their way into the congregation. The worshipers waited to see who would be chosen. Some looked more than a little uneasy. The children took their time in choosing, but when they had made their choice there was no refusing. The children did not speak but simply took the hand of the chosen ones and led them to the front of the sanctuary. Out they came, grannies, dads, and teen-agers. Each child brought one, and Murray thought his point had been well made. He prepared to lead the congregation in a family prayer. However, the children had other plans. Already they were on their way back into the congregation to make another choice.

The front of the sanctuary grew crowded with those who had been led there by the hands of children. Remembering the caution about that congregation's not being used to anything unusual, Murray began to grow anxious. But there was no stopping the children. Back and back they went until they had personally led every worshiper from the pews. The standing worshipers stretched right across the front of the sanctuary, down both side aisles and across the back of the church. Those who had been led to this position by the hand were now holding hands with one another. No one told them to do it. Somehow it must have seemed the most appropriate response to the actions of the children.

For a minute or so, Murray did not know what to do. He looked around that circle of church people who were used to strictly straight worship. No one was frowning. He asked if anyone would like to comment on what had happened. Many people were moved to speak. The last contribution came from a woman who said something like this: "For ages now we have been talking about the need for closer fellowship. But that's what it's mainly been—just talk. Never in my life have I felt as much a part of our church as I do right now. It really does feel like a big family. We always talk about helping our children. This morning our children have helped us." There was a long silence. Finally Murray prayed for the Christian family that was that congregation. When he looked up the circle of hands was still unbroken. There were tears on many cheeks.

On that morning Murray left his prepared sermon on Christian fellowship unpreached. That message had been proclaimed in other ways.

EXPOSITION

Most congregations do occasionally permit children to be seen and heard in some leadership role in worship. However, the nature of their involvement is usually designed and orchestrated by adults. Seldom are children given permission to contribute along the lines of their own insights or in accordance with their own initiatives. This state of affairs does two things. It inhibits the children's appreciation of worship as a celebration of the whole church family, and it cuts the congregation off from an important source of surprising and spontaneous inspiration and challenge.

One of the problems inherent in allowing children to contribute in worship is that of their unpredictability. No one can know in advance what they may say or do. This means that the agenda-oriented, order-of-service-bound ministers or congregations are ill equipped to cope with the contributions of children.

The person and/or congregation who really wants to have the genuine involvement of children must be flexible. There must be a willingness to go with the flow, to look for value in what the children offer. And to keep looking for value even when this offering is something that seems to be off the track. Experience teaches that, given the right environment, children will generally give more than expected and not less. However, only those with eyes to see and ears to hear can recognize the worth of their offerings.

The quality of children's contribution is decided to a large degree by the attitudes of the adults who surround them. Children who above all things like to be liked take a reading on their audience and then give them what they want. Children are not always clowns, but if clowning is what the audience wants, that is what they'll get. The same applies to cuteness. It is no different in matters of wisdom. Children are not fools. Their understandings and interpretations may be different from ours, but from their perspective their words make sense. In fact, when carefully heard, the lateral thinking of children will usually challenge and frequently shed new light on the question or issue under discussion. However, before showing what they really think, our children look for assurance that their words will be respected.

PROPOSITION 20

STARCHILDREN DIE YOUNG.

Lust for Blood

Michelle was born into our family with a beautiful spirit and a handicapped body. We see her beauty, but the world sees her handicap. There is no hiding it. It shows in her face. Nonetheless, her body and brain work well. She is a fully participating member of our family and her school.

We all love vacations. With a tiny plywood trailer in tow, we roll down the back roads of Australia. As we travel through that sunburnt country, our wide land refreshes us. Another day, another camping spot, and so it goes.

We had been in the trailer park for about an hour. Lois and I had chores to do around the trailer. The children were at the swings. Suddenly Michelle appeared without her siblings. She was not crying, she seldom did; but clearly she was upset. We tried to find out what was the matter, but not a word would she say. She simply retreated into the trailer where she lay face down on the bed.

When her younger brother, James, and her younger sister, Cathy, returned, we asked if they knew what had happened. They didn't know everything, but they could tell us enough for us to guess the rest. A group of about seven children, mostly about eight- and nine-year-olds, had spotted Michelle's handicap. At first, they just stared. Then they got to talking and laughing about it among themselves. When Michelle left the swings to go to the bathroom, they followed her, calling out. That was the last James and Cathy had seen of the incident.

It was two days later that Michelle finally told me what happened. As she was close to the bathroom, the jeering band of children closed in on her. She tried to ignore them, but there was no way. They jostled her and then pressed her against the brick wall of the bathroom. She was trapped in a circle of name-calling children. The group's leader pushed her face close to Michelle's. "She called me a living disgrace, Dad. She said I was ugly. Then they all kept saying, 'Smile, come on, pull a face.' " As she told me, she cried softly. Hatred burned in my heart.

Shortly after that, Michelle seemed to forget the incident altogether. I did not. I kept looking at children and trying to identify the kind of child who would do such a thing. When walking with Michelle, I watched for reactions. What I did see was lots of adults staring at my daughter—cold stares, indignant stares, offended stares, even amused stares. I never clarified my mental image of the children who inflicted such violence on my daughter. But I did identify their parents.

EXPOSITION

Christian theological tradition continually draws us back to an awareness that sin must be taken seriously. If we say that we and others are without sin, we are fooling ourselves.

The authors firmly believe that at this point in history the child is in a unique position to give us the gifts of God in a special way. Yet children, as part of the human order, can be instruments of sin. The cruelty of children is legendary.

Students of child development confirm the early impact of the culture upon this creature hot from the heart of God.

The biology, psychology, sociology, and theology of parents, family, and culture are all working on that freshly born life. Whether it is the curse of Eden or the wickedness of the current human condition that spoils God's freshest creation, our thesis is not challenged. God has always used sinners as special messengers with special revelations.

Starchildren are also sinners. However, it is the grace of God in Jesus Christ that enables them to be special messengers. Their blessing is that they innocently present precious facets of his Good News in spite of themselves. It is the growing self-consciousness of these gifts that marks the slipping away of the Starchild qualities.

The reason children can speak so directly to the church is that it is possible for adults to read these special qualities so easily in the child. Yet some adults do not seem equipped with ears to hear and eyes to see. They either confuse lapses into childish behavior with Starchild qualities or they become overly sentimental about the "cute" characteristics of children.

The authors are neither sentimental nor unaware of the trials of the childish side of children.

However, the redemptive act of God in Jesus Christ empowers the adult to receive the gifts the child offers in a unique fashion. The jewel of God qualities in our Starchildren can be experienced by gently bathing its facets in the light of hope and forgiveness.

PROPOSITION 21

STARCHILDREN LOVE THEMSELVES AND OTHERS.

I Am Such a Nice Person

One of the few advantages of being away from the family is that your children write you letters. I keep all of them with care. Each year they grow more valuable to all of us.

Cathy writes great letters. She never has submitted to the idea that you write a letter with words only. Drawings of faces, flowers, and comical animals have always been an important part of her correspondence. Before reading the words of Cathy's letters, the reader is already attracted to the artwork.

When she was seven, she wrote to me about her part in a Sunday school dramatic presentation. Her assessment of her own performance was straightforward and to the point: "I was very good and everybody liked me." She went on to conclude her five-line letter with her thoughts about me. "I love you lots, Daddy. I miss you. Come home soon." Then there were lots of hugs and kisses.

EXPOSITION

I was raised on a style of Christianity that had lots to say about the sin of pride. Yet clearly my own daughter had a very high opinion of herself. If I had still been under that kind of rigid, old-time religion, this evidence could have suggested to me that she was far from the Kingdom. My opinion now is quite the reverse. I cannot believe that my daughter's unselfconscious affirmation of her own worth was a sign of sinfulness. Rather, I take it as evidence that she is one of those to whom Jesus referred when he said, "Of such are the kingdom of heaven."

Behind a large number of attempted and successful suicides, behind numerous psychosomatic diseases, behind multitudes of broken relationships, lies an inability to love oneself. Some just so afflicted are beautiful people, some are unattractive people, some are overweight people, and some are athletic people. All kinds and conditions of persons are included who have difficulty feeling good about themselves. The reasons vary, but most go back to early childhood experiences. Whatever the cause, to go on living with such feelings is to be vulnerable to inner disruption and, for some, destruction.

Babies, toddlers, and children can help us be free of the binds of inappropriate humility and debilitating self-rejection. While we play games about who we are and what we can do, they tell us about themselves straight from the shoulder. We should seek to listen and learn from the child who publicly owns his strengths and will speak openly about his abilities. To discourage this behavior would be a sin. To allow them to encourage these affirmations in us is to be moved in the direction of health. It would be a gross distortion if it were thought that this assertion is an encouragement to crude bragging or boasting. To brag is to exaggerate. To go on and on is to boast. But to quietly and clearly affirm our own worth and skills is to give evidence of the life of the Starchild within us.

There is a connection between Cathy's ability to say "I love you lots" and her own feeling of self-worth. Without self-appreciation there can be no appreciation of others.

PROPOSITION 22

STARCHILDREN
TASTE AND KNOW
THAT THE LORD IS GOOD.

Yum, Yum, Good

A bloodcurdling scream came through the door. It was a strange sound. There wasn't pain or hatred in the shrill human cry. The scream sounded like a primitive language.

Brian was jumping up and down in the hospital crib. His eyes danced as he saw me. More high-pitched sounds filled the room. I was struck by the sight before me. The small child had been in the children's ward for several months. His disfigured face was slowly healing. More skin grafts would follow to restore parts of the face. There was little hope for his vocal cords.

Brian had let his childish curiosity lead him to near self-destruction. He had ingested drain-cleaner crystals, and his saliva activated the acid.

Every parent worries about such tragedies. There are so many chemicals that endanger life and health in the medicine cabinets and cleaning closets. Such doors must be locked because a child must touch and taste to learn and grow, the ready lips and tongue primed for every part of the expanding world.

Toddler Amy was playing with a toy horn. She started stumbling across the room with the instrument in her mouth. Instantly, her mother knew what was going to happen. She could only wince as the child tumbled to the floor. The mouthpiece jammed into her throat. Blood spurted out of her mouth. Amy screamed, and Marilyn did what she could to comfort the frightened child. It was imperative that they rush to the doctor.

The clinic was quick in handling the case. The doctor concluded that most of the bleeding had stopped. Just a bit deeper and Amy would have lost her tonsils. "Give her liquids, but don't let her have any solids for a day or so."

As the family sat eating that night, Amy seemed resigned to her temporary fast. Yet she looked intently at the dining family. We could see the hunger and the longing for the taste of food. She reached out and took a piece of bread. Amy held it for a minute. Then she pushed it into the mouth of her father. She was tasting the goodness of food through the feeding of another.

A long time had passed in our relationship before Bill asked if he could go to church with me. We had worked through some very heavy things. This teen-ager had known many abuses in his short life. He had been beaten and neglected as a child. Yet the miracle of love had brought him to a point when he wanted to know more about the celebration of faith.

I was pleased that he would be attending the church on a Communion Sunday. What a wondrous way to experience some of the most vital aspects of the gospel! The pastor was quite compelling as he proclaimed the hope of the Lord's table.

As we walked home, Bill reflected on the service and what he had experienced. He noted that hospitality had been absent. "Only the ushers said something to me."

I asked about the Communion service. He questioned me

about the strange little squares that had been used for Communion. He smiled. "They promised the body of Christ. All they delivered was fish food."

EXPOSITION

The lips and tongue of the newborn babe are keys to the child's survival. To taste and suck ensures that life will continue. The importance of oral satisfaction extends into adulthood.

Yet the senses are threatening for most religious folk. Some traditions have preserved biblical appreciation for touching, tasting, smelling, seeking, and hearing. However, the kiss of peace is rarely that in most of our liturgical settings.

We have been restricting our sensual input of celebrating the faith to hearing and unstimulating viewing. There is little concern with touching, smelling, and tasting.

Our most accessible sensual experience is tasting. The Communion service or Mass provides an opportunity to taste and see that God is good. It is too easy to approach the Lord's table with either complacency or too much reverence. It is the Starchild who leads us to enjoy the Table and glorify the God of the feast. The child loves the party and the celebration.

Folk who have responded to the Starchild presence in Communion have found a source of renewal for the people of God. In one setting the children accompanied the adults to the Communion rail. Although this tradition did not permit small children to partake, they were present with the parent. The priest would serve the elements, then place his hands on each child, and bless him or her. There were smiles and energy around the table. The pastor claims that the whole service is now enriched through the contributions of the children.

Starchildren value highly their sense of taste. What is natural for them has grown stale for most adults. Let the sensitivity of these taste buds lead others to know God more completely.

PROPOSITION 23

SICK STARCHILDREN CAN LIVE.

Eyes like Wolves

About one hundred fifty people from six different parishes attended the celebration. As each group brought some new thing to the worship, the occasion grew in its meaning and power. It seemed that everything was leading up to that final love feast. If all went as planned, it could be a joyful culmination of our afternoon together. It was only as the table was being set that I had my first premonition of trouble.

The people whose job it was to arrange the food had gone to a lot of trouble. The freshly peeled fruit, marshmallows, cookies, and white and dark chocolates were set out like a work of art. There was not a lot of anything, but there was enough for everyone to have at least one item. This was to be a symbolic party. We were trying to make the point that good parties cannot be measured in accordance with the amount of food or drink consumed. All this sounds good in theory, but I suddenly became aware that it may never work. As I looked around our gathering, I could see thirty or so small children who were with us staring at the chocolates on the table. Some who were sitting on the floor were already beginning to wriggle their way closer to the table. Their eyes were like wolves.

I had an awful feeling that I knew what was about to happen. As soon as I said "Go" or even before, those children would be scrambling for the chocolates. And not just one but as many as they could grasp. I guessed that some of those who were now inching toward the table were even ready to fight for possession. Looking around I could see that some adults were smiling. Perhaps they were thinking, "Kids and chocolates, what a combination! How cute." I felt sick to the stomach.

All I could do was talk. I reminded the whole group how on that afternoon our bonds of love in Christ had turned strangers into family. I talked about how we were to have this special meal, a kind of a party that could sum up our whole afternoon together. "A good party," I said, "does not depend on how much you eat but on who you eat it with and how you eat it." I pointed out that there really was only enough for everyone to take one thing. "That's OK," I said, "because the secret of this party is sharing, and that's going to be just about the best part." I talked about how sad Jesus would be if his people were greedy. I said: "A wonderful thing is going to happen here this afternoon. We are going to see how with just a few provisions, we will have the greatest party."

The miracle happened. The children sat quiet and still. They waited their turn. They took their one goodie and, with all due courtesy, served their neighbors. And as for the leftovers, the children took the plates and served the adults first before serving one another. Parents were amazed. I was relieved. The wolf in the children's eyes had been replaced with a lamb. It nearly didn't happen. In a way, under the Holy Spirit, I had been a doctor in bringing health back to ailing Starchildren.

EXPOSITION

The events of that meal led to long conversations with parents. One parent had told me that he had believed that it was either unwise or impossible to restrain children. That is, they were wolfish by nature, and that wolfishness must be expressed. All the adults could do was watch with the best humor possible. Another parent talked of what he felt to be a dominant assumption in our society. He said: "Nowadays we show our love to our children by giving them more. To do anything less than to give them all they want is to deprive the child of a birthright." According to this attitude, he said, "our children measure our love by how much we give them." Both parents were now questioning these assumptions.

Greed kills Starchildren. It can destroy them at nine, it can disfigure them at four, it can mar them at two. Here we are not talking about that natural life-preserving selfishness and separation that are essential parts of growing up. Rather, it is that lust for more and more things. It is that pushing, screaming, kicking, and biting approach to life that flavors so much of the adult world.

Starchildren are aware of a more gentle spirit. This book documents something of that special spirit. But Starchildren are open to being subverted and perverted by the spirit of the culture and mores of our society. It is inevitable that eventually they will be molded by these pressures. But the extent to which this happens and the speed at which it happens is largely determined by the persons who surround the Starchild. These significant persons can nurture and encourage the Starchild's gentle and generous spirit and so keep at bay the heart of the wolf. "It all came to me in a flash," said one of the fathers, "as I watched those kids just aching to get a handful of those chocolates. That's us out there. That's our world and those are our values. 'Give me, give me, give me. And I'll push you out of the way to get it.' Those attitudes hold no hope for any of us. My goodness, if we don't stop thinking that way, it will kill us all." The heart of every Starchild knows this to be the truth.

PROPOSITION 24

STARCHILDREN ARE THE FRUITS
OF GOD'S FORGIVENESS.

Tut, Tut

The clinic was designed to provide families with the help they need for mental health. The waiting rooms had been structured to provide a suitable holding area for the whole family.

The small boy was taking advantage of the environment. He had commandeered the chalkboard. With colored chalk he had drawn his creative impression of a train. The thirty minutes of work produced an imaginative impression of energy, speed, and mystery.

The boy's father stepped over to the board. In a loud voice he started pointing out the mistakes his son had made in the art piece. With one hand he erased the misplaced wheels, the disproportionate smokestack. He then proceeded to draw realistic versions of these features.

At first the boy offered a mild protest but soon fell silent as he noticed that the whole room was focusing on this criticism by his dad: "Now that is the way that it should have been. I have made it correct for you. Did you understand your mistakes?" The boy quietly dropped into a chair and just looked off into space.

It had been one of those weeks when things hadn't worked out. That was true of work, and it was true of home and, of course, the kids got mixed up in it as well. They seemed to have been even more untidy than normal and had managed to forget or only half complete most of their chores. They were pulled into line on all these things in language loud and clear.

It seemed like just another mealtime. It was when Lois left the table to fix the dessert that I first got the feeling that something was up. My three children were strangely quiet. They were fidgeting, pushing, and poking one another. It was something different from the usual run of mealtime teasing. They had something on their minds.

"Dad," James spoke. All eyes were on me. Straightaway, I knew it was a put-up job. It had all been planned. Yielding to his sisters' pressure, James was to be their spokesman. "Dad," he said, "we've got something to ask you."

"Go ahead."

"Dad, when you were a kid did you ever do any-thing—wrong? I mean, did you ever do any naughty things?"

They say that at some moments of crisis all your life flashes before your eyes. Well, in that moment a thousand images of my parenting crowded my brain. And they were all bad. "Oh, glory!" I thought. "What kind of a picture of myself have I been putting out? And whatever have I been telling the kids about themselves?" I thought of all that time and energy given to do's and don'ts and reprimands. Always acting the person in the right, the one who's been offended, the one who is aggrieved. Those poor little kids. They've seen me acting the hurt hero, and they're beginning to wonder if they're not the naughtiest kids in the world.

EXPOSITION

Jesus has warned us about judging others. However, the parental, caretaker approach we take in our relationship with children often forces us into such negative judgmental roles. After all, how can people learn without being corrected? This assumption didn't work for us and certainly doesn't work with our children.

John 8 may have had a shaky textual history; however, the spirit of Christ is captured beautifully in this story. It is not Jesus who joins the crowd in the orgy of judging. The woman caught in adultery knows her sin. But it is the One who stands with her who frees her to sin no more.

The church's treatment of Starchildren has been based on such a judgmental approach. It is easier to correct the young than to participate with them in a mutual ministry of reconciliation.

The Epistle of James encourages us to confess to one another. This does not mean that the adult wears the judicial robes to try the child for mistakes. It suggests that we experience the forgiveness of Christ in community with others.

Many adults try to live as if they were not sinners. They simply suppress the truth. Others turn to therapists for the acts of confession and pardon. This is not good enough for the community of faith. The Starchildren open the adult community to a refreshing opportunity to restore its talking relationship to God. The child brings forgiveness and seeks forgiveness. It is this symbiotic relationship that is so fresh and new.

We have often focused on the heroes of the Bible and contemporary life as we teach children. Yet the whole biblical story is based on the fact that God uses sinners. An honest child knows that he or she is always making mistakes and doing wrong. How can such a little one possibly relate to a superhero? We have to provide the real biblical and social models of faith. All of God's servants are sinners. This includes Mom and Dad. Yet we are forgiven sinners.

The child's vulnerability is the gift. As we reach out to be agents of forgiveness and pardon, so we receive these gifts in abundance from the child. The Starchild is the seal of God's acceptance and love.

Fred Rogers helps us recapture the Good News concerning the mistakes of the child. "I like you just the way you are." This good man knows that the gospel is also fine psychology. It is affirmation that breeds responsibility and a sense of self-worth.

The child loses the forgiveness of God as the adult points out his or her wrongdoings. The adult unwittingly creates the impression that the older generation is without sin.

It is only through receiving the gift of forgiveness of sins from the Starchild that we know God's forgiveness.

In the liturgical context, Protestants often do not deal adequately with forgiveness. The sinful people gather to worship and depart with the same garbage bottled up inside. A few phrases read from the pulpit do not forgiveness make. The reality of God's forgiveness must be incarnate in our lives.

PROPOSITION 25

STARCHILDREN SEE VISIONS.

Sharp Eyes

The slide showed a little three- or four-year-old girl. She was holding a fairly large, oval mirror. In the mirror she could see her own reflection. Her face was alight with the smile of one who was pleased with what she saw. This one slide was projected onto a daylight screen positioned over the Communion table. It became a dominating visual image for our Easter service.

The Easter service proceeded with the Resurrection readings and the appropriate hymns and prayers. Just prior to the sermon, I directed the congregation's attention to the slide. Prior to this I had made no reference to her; but as we read and prayed, she smiled on. I asked the congregation to think for a moment about why I had chosen that slide as a visual focus on Easter. After a minute of silence, I asked folk to share the meanings that came to them.

Our people found lots of Easter messages in that slide. Some saw the happiness of the Resurrection. Others thought it spoke to them of the vitality of new life. Messages about rebirth were also shared. I was about to close the sharing when someone pointed out a little girl with her hand up. "I think I know why you're showing us that slide on Easter Day," she said. "Because Jesus died for our sins and rose again, we can look in the mirror and smile." She had said it all. The more I think about it, the more I am convinced that that really is the essence of the joy of resurrection morning. However, I doubt that I could have put it so simply.

EXPOSITION

Children are not usually able to understand sermons. They have difficulty joining discussions on abstract themes. They are poorly equipped for participating in dialogue that requires wide experience. However, children are not at a disadvantage when it comes to creating and interpreting art forms.

Children are masters of imagination. Faces in clouds, jungles in backyards, changing dogs into horses and the family car into a space vehicle; it's all stock-in-trade for the average child.

The adult perception is directed toward seeing things as they are. And while this should not preclude viewing life with imagination, unfortunately it often does.

To live without imagination is like living with black and white images in a colorful world. And there is more involved than this. The person who only sees things as they are has lost the capacity to see things as they may be. The artist, the poet, the creative person in every realm is that way because he or she has clung to and developed the gift of imagination.

Increasingly, the church is rediscovering the value of visual communication. Ancient symbols are being dusted down and looked at again. All kinds of contemporary groups are discovering that as they strive to create new symbols they become involved in doing their own theology. Congregations are handing around rocks and flowers and pieces of junk. Worshipers are finding exciting new meanings in everyday objects. Slides of scenes, street signs, and people are being used in worship to stimulate and facilitate prayer and meditation.

As we move into this world of visual inspiration, our children can come with us. In this sphere they are equal partners. Seeing imaginatively is their thing, finding meaning in unlikely objects is what they do every day. As we ponder the visual symbol, their sharp eyes will pick up things ours miss. They can do great things for us. Starchildren can take people who are locked into the black and white world of the secular society and lead them into the technicolor world of God's promises. That is, if we will let them.

PROPOSITION 26

STARCHILDREN ARE SUFFERING SERVANTS.

Hold My Hand

"I can't believe how insensitive people are to those who may look a bit different. My son has a genetic condition that causes his head to grow faster than the rest of his body.

"One day my son and I were walking through an amusement park. We were holding hands. I was stunned by the reactions of adults. People would stop and bend over him and look him up and down like they were examining a piece of meat in the store.

"I could only hold on to his hand tightly and make him know that he belonged to me and that I was proud to be related to him."

"At a picnic with friends there was a five-year-old who acted like a Yorkshire terrier, and she had curls down the front of her head. She couldn't understand why my severely retarded daughter was bigger than she but couldn't talk as well.

"It really bothered her. I went to a lot of trouble to explain to her that my daughter's brain is different from hers. 'Well, how old is she?'

"I said, 'Well, she is eight, but not a regular eight.' The little girl thought and thought on that. She worked it over and over in her mind. Later that evening we were sitting by the volleyball area when she came over to me. The little girl looked at me for a couple of minutes.

" 'Don't you wish Deanna was a regular eight?'

"I said, 'Sure we do. But everybody can't be a regular eight.'

"The fact that that child of five years understood how we felt gives you strength to hope that maybe someone a little older will understand."

It had been one of those special outings. I had organized the day camps as a way the church could serve the children and families of our community. It was all quite simple. The buses were rented and the volunteers were recruited. The mix of adult and teen-aged staff members was just what I desired. During our orientation I underscored the fact that these children had much to give to all of us.

The five days went very smoothly. After the last session, we were reflecting on what had happened in the course of the week.

One of the teen-agers on our staff had been in a lot of trouble. He had actually spent some time in detention. It was quite clear that he had been greatly moved by this experience with children. "One of the little girls came over to me one day and took my hand. Can you imagine? Someone actually turning to me for help?"

EXPOSITION

Starchildren have enormous staying power in their quest for understanding and caring. In the early days of star power, they seem able to survive in the most dehumanizing context. Yet the hurt takes its toll.

Starchildren have a wholistic perception of the world. It all fits together in their strange and primitive logic.

The warm squeeze of a hand may convince them that this is a person who can really help. A smile can wipe away the pain inflicted by the cruel ones. An adult's loving participation in a question or problem is enough to make it all clear for the young ones.

In the process of this quest for comfort and peace, our tiny folk give a great deal. They enable the more mature to experience hope, responsibility, and importance. These gifts are precious to those dwelling in a world short on such commodities.

Instead of protecting the young from the challenges of the harsh culture, we must let them lead us directly into confrontation with it. Starchildren do not take us to fantasy land. They challenge us to face reality. It is our emotional kinship that makes it possible for young and old to face the same problems in the same ways.

Religion has been drifting along with secular culture in many circles. The escapism of nostalgia is simply not compatible with the biblical faith. We cannot buy or dream a world of peace and love. The child is the person who feels the end result of the pressures of the world. This smallest of human creatures is the ultimate victim of our harshness, selfishness, and cruelty.

Starchildren are capable of facing the worst and the hardest of life. Yet their need to reach out to us during these trials is their gift to the adult. It is this community of suffering that validates the Christian community at its best and most faithful. The capacity to understand suffering and to suffer may be the Starchild's greatest ministry to the church.

PROPOSITION 27

STARCHILDREN GATHER THE TRIBE.

In the Name of the Father, Son, and Holy Ghost

It was hot and humid. The small church was packed with warm bodies. As I looked over the congregation I caught the rhythm of paper fans moving slowly back and forth.

The pastor had urged me to share my work with youth. I used several short bits of conversation from a friend who used and sold heroin. The audio material had been cued on my cassette recorder so that it was available over the sound system at the touch of my finger. I asked the worshipers to follow me as I walked and talked with my young friend. His pain and confusion were overwhelming. There were many misty eyes at the end of the service.

During informal coffee hour that followed, a young woman emerged from the circle of twenty people. She carried a very young baby in her arms. "I was very moved by the story of Tom." I wasn't ready for what happened next. She looked at her baby and began to cry. "How can I raise him to have a good life? How can I be sure that he doesn't get carried away like your young friend?"

Everyone stopped talking. This was a closely knit church. When one part of its body suffers, everyone else feels it. The people closed in around us. The young woman continued, "I had him baptized last week. How can I live up to those vows?"

I looked around at the folk in the room. One older man walked over and took the baby from the woman. He held the child for a few seconds. Gently rocking him in his arms he spoke. "Jenny, we—the members of the church took some vows last week also. It will be hard for you, but you will do your best. It may even be harder for us to remember how this baby is part of our family and needs our care, but we're sure gonna try. We love you both. Maybe with God's help we can all make it."

EXPOSITION

There is a temptation in many churches to run all the baptism/dedications of babies together as a mass event. There is probably some idea of time economy behind such scheduling. However, these rites of passage are moments of great importance to the whole community.

The Starchild at his or her most helpless stage provides an occasion for reaffirmation of faith for all concerned. To be recommitted to the responsibility of caring for a member of the household of faith is vital to the adult.

We are living in a time when there are many single parents. The broken and bruised body of Christ is reflected in the wounds of the young and the old who are survivors of families on the rocks.

The three to five minutes when a child is formally recognized as being part of the faith family and the adults acknowledge their responsibility to the child is an act of grace. Each person deserves that moment of receiving and giving love. Many church families are now giving these rites their due. The presence of babies in worship is one of the most vital symbols of God's grace.

The ministry of the community to and with parents of young children is extremely important and within the scope of every church. This vast extended family of Christ is something very special in our fragmented society.

Parenting and godparenting are special arts that are a true concern of the church. The Starchild's needs become an occasion for the diverse members of the faith family to give.

The congregation is filled with special people who have the experience and concern to support the new parents in the task of nurture. Perhaps all we have to do is give our folk permission to become involved in the lives of others in a natural manner.

The Starchild is not just a cute footnote in the service of worship. He or she is a herald of the Good News. As we gather with the young family, we again experience the possibility of glorifying God and enjoying him forever.

WE HAVE STOOD

Well, the madness of putting these thoughts together has come to an end. Dennis and Stan have run, slept, and eaten around this project. Families—present and absent—have moved in and out of our lives as we have written. They have massaged our message as we worked.

Many of the kind folk mentioned at the beginning of the book were helpful as they peeked over our shoulders and vigorously reacted to the life we have tried to assemble on the printed page.

The authors of this work come out of this project better friends than ever. The Starchild qualities have flamed up again and burn within us in a new way.

As we labored two things became clear. One was that we were raising many questions that we had to leave unanswered. The second was that, despite this unfinished aspect, we felt the need to make our statement to the church concerning the ministry of the child. We have tried to do this with as much faithfulness and strength as we could muster.

We would love to share your experiences in the quest to be young again. Write us. Stan is found near Post Office Box 124, Warrandyte, Victoria 3113, Australia; and Dennis hangs out around Post Office Box 12811, Pittsburgh, Pennsylvania 15241.

May the spirit of God continue to give you rebirth. May he bless you with the company and ministry of Starchildren.

USER'S GUIDE PART I

A SIX-SESSION COURSE FOR GROUP STUDY

How to Put It Together

In this section the authors have designed a six-week course for adults concerning the ministry of the child in the radical transformation of the faith community. We have focused on the kinds of things the group can experience about the possibilities revealed in the ministry of children.

You will notice that the sessions are developed according to the spirit of the child. In other words, there will be a meandering flow of experiences, idea, and insights. We ask you to join in this kind of learning environment. It will mean that you must trust your feelings in considering when your folk are ready to move on to something else. On the other hand, there will be times when you might spend the whole time on just one particular focus that has caught the imagination of the group. The child helps us understand and appreciate the value of this nonlinear approach to life. It is a marvelous context for releasing the strengths and energies of your people.

We also hope that you will examine the options open to you for conducting this course in different settings and time slots. For instance, this offering might provide just the right kind of course for a Lenten series, or perhaps your church has had some good experiences with camps or retreats. This material would work very well in such a weekend setting. The course material could also be altered to fit a Sunday-morning format.

The authors believe that the course will work best if there is a contract among the members of the group. In other words, the group should make a covenant to participate fully and faithfully as sharing members for the full six weeks. The enabler of the group can draw up an actual statement of commitment. Write it on newsprint and have everyone sign it.

The Nature of It

Each week has a theme. Each introductory focus is supported by an Old Testament and a New Testament passage. We firmly believe that the historical and theological foundation for the probe of our concept must be rooted in the Bible. Theological study is richest when various texts can be appreciated. However, the actual application and placement of the texts will vary from session to session. It is the spirit of the passages that gives you the security to undertake this quest.

There are three parts to each session. The first aspect is the gathering experience. This section utilizes a symbolic sharing that may be nonverbal. It grows out of the theme and the context.

The second part is the group experience. This thrust may flow from the opening (or gathering). It may involve the reading of selections from the book.

The third aspect is the parting. This portion of the session will also carry liturgical overtones in keeping with the opening. As the group moves from the experience, there will be a set of tasks for the next time. This dimension of the parting is very important. The assignments will contain the stimuli for action, if that should be the option of the group.

It is important to note that the course is not designed to lead people into learning certain facts. We are inviting people to learn about themselves, their experiences, and the children within and without themselves. We commission them to go out into their congregations in the spirit of dialogue and exploration. We challenge them to confront the hard and happy news concerning children. There will be no right or wrong conclusions to these probes. Of course, we do hope that the students will entertain the possibility that God has blessed young and old children with important gifts for all.

We are drawing heavily upon the importance of symbols in our lives. Humans are artifact-collecting, symbol-creating beings. It is sad that the commercial world has stepped in and fed these needs more completely than the faith community. Yet Christ committed us forever to the serious probing of symbols by his act of breaking the bread and offering the cup. Let the Spirit flow through your people as they explore the symbolic dimension of these sessions. The power of such moments will surprise you. Don't rush through something that has unexpected importance. Don't let an agenda detract from such moments. God will use your people in this quest for the truth.

We are assuming that the group will number about twenty people. However, if you have a larger group, simply adjust the guidelines accordingly. You can easily work in smaller units too. Just divide the group into working sections, and have these folk report their work to the whole group.

We are also suggesting that each of your class members keep a journal throughout the six-week or weekend experience. A small notebook will serve well. Each of the sessions will provide plenty of opportunity for writing. The assignments can be recorded in this way. Also encourage your folk to record daily their feelings as they probe the contribution of the child within themselves.

The Ministry of Children

If you have worked your way through the book, you will be familiar with our thesis. We feel that God has touched the children among us and within us in a special way. These gifts are for the faith community. It is possible to draw upon these gifts within us. Yet it is the natural child who is immediately in touch with these attributes. *The course is probing the assumption that children have a vital ministry to the church.*

More and More

This course is only one of the resources of this User's Guide. Part II contains some clues for using the course as a nurture of new parents and those who have had their children baptized/dedicated. Perhaps some from your course could teach it again for those folk who need and deserve the continual support of the community.

You will also note that the User's Guide, Part II, contains a model for a family worship experience that could provide the climax for your course. Please entertain the possibility of such an event. The results of using this model have been exciting.

The Six-Week Course

Session One

Theme: Creation
Texts: Genesis 1:1-5
         II Corinthians 5:17-20
Materials: A safety pin for each member of the course
             A baby blanket

Copies of: *The Ministry of the Child*
                      Propositions 2, 8, 14, 21, and 27

1. *The development and execution of the covenant among the members of the course.*

2. *Gathering of the learning community.* Your aim here is to get in touch with feelings evoked by articles surrounding human birth. Use a blanket to which is pinned one safety pin for each class member. Gather the group in a tight circle and pass the prepared blanket while encouraging each person to experience it fully (touch, snuggle, smell). Then ask each person to share the memories evoked by the blanket.

3. *Group experience.* Divide the group so that each unit has one of the proposition sections to read. Ask them to focus on the stories. Have them make notes in their journals if these are used.

The leader then reads Genesis 1:1-5. Have the whole group discuss places where the stories may touch themes presented by the biblical material. This may be a simple word association or more complete kind of response. Let your people make the points of contact.

4. *Parting of the community.* At this point in the learning experience you will want to return to the opening process with the blanket. Have your folk gather in the circle. Once again pass the baby's wrap around the group, and ask each person to remove a safety pin.

Let each person hold the pin in his or her hand during a few moments of silent reflection on memories evoked from their childhood. Encourage them to think about the feelings stirring within them.

Then ask each person to share a word or a sentence that is triggered by the object held. The enabler then might make a few comments about how one of the functions of the safety pin is to hold things together.

Ask the group to share ideas about how children hold

families and societies together. After these comments have been made, read II Corinthians 5:17-20. Note that reconciliation (binding together) is one of the key ministries of Jesus.

5. *Assignment: doing the faith.* Suggest that during the week each person scan the newspapers and magazines for signs of the promise of God to hold things together through children. Each person is to bring back one clipping that seems to show that sin has threatened God's promise of reconciliation. The final act of the group should be an act of pinning the safety pin on your clothing. This pin is a sign of your covenant and should be brought back every week. Also ask your folk to read Propositions 6, 12, 24, and 14 for the next session.

OR

You might want to undertake the group experience of using the art forms of creation so appreciated by children. Clay, finger painting, blocks, and construction paper are some easy supplies to be used in this setting.

You might explain after the reading of Genesis 1:1-5 that some early translations of the passage used the word *beautiful* where *good* appears. This provides some exciting ways of viewing creation. The term *good* has an ethical or legal feel about it. *Beautiful* on the other hand, suggests an aesthetic thrust. Perhaps we should be living as artists rather than as judges. Then ask them to create something that captures the awe and beauty of creation. These arts can then be shared in relationship to the stories and the Genesis passage.

Session Two

Theme: Sin and Forgiveness
Texts: Psalm 51:1-4
         I John 1:5-10
Materials: A few of last week's newspapers (for those who forget)

Basins or bowls of water
Cakes of hand soap
Cloth towels
Paste and poster board (or bulletin board and
    thumb tacks)
Propositions 6, 12, 24, 14

1. *Gathering of the learning community.* Gather in a circle and ask people for their clippings of things that seem to challenge God's holding the world together through children. These are placed on the floor in the center of the circle. Ask group members to pick up someone else's clipping and to read and contemplate it. Then have a time of sharing in which group members explain and respond to the article they have just chosen.

After all have shared, have a time of general reflection on the total input. The leader can help the group reflect on the implications of these comments in the light of last week's study on creation. Why has the creation that started in hope and promise become so grubby for the youngest? Then have people pick out a clipping and pin it on another person, using that person's safety pin. The leader can then read the passage from I John.

2. *Group experience.* Have the members of the class form duos. Give each duo a few minutes to focus on signs of sin found within the clippings both are wearing. At what points are we personally part of this sin? Then spend some time struggling to find signs of hope within these bad situations. Have each duo list these signs of grace. How can they personally or in their church participate in bringing hope out of the midst of sin?

3. *Parting.* This act of forgiveness and healing is quite important. You will want to use several bowls of water. Have your folk gather around the bowls and take turns washing the hands of one another. Use a bar of hand soap and the towels for this act. The leader might want to read

Psalm 51:1-4 at this point. As a person finishes washing and being washed, he or she can go to the bulletin board or poster board and put up his or her clipping depicting sin.

4. *Assignments.* While wearing the safety pin, each member is to approach a person under six or over sixty. Each is to witness about his or her symbol to the other person. In the course of these discussions the students are to ask some questions: If you were God, what would be the most pleasing part of creation to you? If you were God looking down at the creation, what would you change?

The most satisfying way of doing this assignment is to have the answers recorded on cassette tapes. The people being interviewed will be pleased at this special attention. It is also a good way to share material in the next session. You will want to ask those who do the recording to limit the tape they share to two minutes. If this method is not chosen, encourage your folk to use their journals. The results will be shared next week. Have them also read Propositions 9, 25, 15, 5, 10, and 11 before next meeting.

Close the session by holding hands and offering a simple prayer. The leader can pick up the fact of the clean hands. There is great affirmation in the fact that God in Jesus Christ has cleansed us of all unrighteousness.

OR

If your folk are more adventuresome, you might have a traveling lesson. Make arrangements to go to a child or a teen-age shelter in your community. Don't just talk to the staff, but try to spend some time with the children and teen-agers. Close your session at the shelter in the manner suggested above.

Session Three

Theme: Rebirth
Texts: John 3:1-8
         Exodus 3:1-14

Materials: One candle
              Propositions 9, 25, 15, 5, 10, and 11

1. *Gathering of the community.* A good deal of time can be spent debriefing the rich experiences your folk will have had in their discussions with people over sixty or under six. You might first start with the reactions they got to the safety-pin witness. How did it feel to be marked with this sign of the child? Work in triads. Have each person share experiences of the interviews with the over-sixty or under-six with the others in his or her trio. These stories are to be summarized on newsprint in one word or key phrase for the whole group.

2. *Group experience.* Each person is to sort out the three things that most urgently need to be done in the world facing the child. Have them record these on the pages of their journals. When this task is completed, the leader should write on a blank sheet the following: Dear God, I would like to have you help me with the following problems. Each person should write an honest letter to God. When this has been done, people should be encouraged to share either the letters or the feelings they had while writing the letters.

3. *The parting.* Gather the group in a circle and place a lighted candle in the middle. The leader can create the atmosphere for reflection by sharing how the candle suggests new life and light. Read John 3:1-8, and remind the group that rebirth means becoming childlike again. Have the folk in the circle share the childlike qualities that need to be rekindled in them. Perhaps the session could end by singing a child's hymn ("Jesus Loves Me," etc.) and/or a child's prayer.

4. *Assignment.* Ask your folk to get in touch with their own suffering as a child. They are to share this pain next week through a mime, picture, body movement, tape, or some other art form. The object is to communicate the hurtful moment.

OR

You might borrow from a local library a film that shows the birth of a child. This could be used in the session as you explore rebirth as related to childlike qualities. If you use this approach, you might consider a rite of birth used by some cultures. The person being initiated as an adult passes between the legs of other adults as they stand in a long line over the crawling person. The symbolic birth could be used very nicely in settings such as weekend events.

Session Four

Theme: Suffering and Healing
Texts: Isaiah 53:1-3
       John 3:16
Materials: Propositions 3, 17, 18, 20, and 26
      Vaseline or slightly scented salve

1. *Gathering of the people.* Take the time to give each person one minute to share through creative acts (mime, body movement, pictures, poetry, dance, etc.) the hurts from their own childhood.

2. *Group experience.* Have the folk form small groups. Share how those childhood hurts were healed. Then ask in what ways a child helped in the healing, or what childlike qualities brought a sense of wholeness again. Anoint one another with the salve.

OR

You might want to focus on the story in Proposition 20. This powerful story deals with suffering and healing. The group can be divided into three units. One unit will assume the emotional identity of Michelle's parents. The second unit will represent the child who has abused Michelle. The two units are to face each other. What do they say or do? The last group has the role of parents whose child has inflicted this hurt. The groups may want to role play the situation.

3. *Assignment.* Ask your folk to talk with a person either

under six years old or over sixty. Pick a different aged person from the one talked to last time. This time ask the person to lend you an object of meaning. Ask the person why the ring, vase, rock, or other object is an important symbolic extension of that person. Witness to the importance of your safety pin and leave that with the person as a symbol of good faith. Your folk will share these objects and stories with the group at the next session.

Session Five

Theme: Community of Saints
Texts: I Corinthians 12:14-26
          Exodus 3:15-16
Materials: Loaf of bread
             Propositions 9, 19, 22, 23, 27

1. *Gathering of the community.* Have your people share the stories of the people they met and show the objects they brought with them. Place each object in the circle during the sharing. Leave them there until the conclusion of the session. After the sharing, read I Corinthians 12:14-26. Encourage your folk to try to bring all these different parts together into one meaningful statement of faith. You might do this by having them arrange the objects on the floor into a total design that reflects the wholeness of Christ's body. Let your folk work on this.

2. *Breadboard.* This feast is to be a celebration of the tension between our brokenness and our wholeness. Pass the loaf, and ask each person to share a thought about some person (living or dead) who is remembered by the eating of the loaf. These members of the communion of saints can be both young and old. Read Exodus 3:15-16. Take a couple of minutes to reflect on how you are going to return the important object to the person who lent it. Should the group pray for them? Would a symbolic gift be fitting? Could you share how this study group prayed for them? These saints

have let you have an important part of themselves. This is a very dear sharing. Close with a prayer circle.

OR

You might want to bring the people who have shared their objects. This would take some planning. It could be a very rewarding celebration of the communion of saints.

3. *Assignments.* Divide the group, and assign each unit one of the four areas of the local church's life: fellowship, learning, worship, and mission. Ask them to analyze that particular area in the light of how successful they have been at bringing to it the Starchild qualities. Before the next session this will require interviews, conversations, a perusal of bulletins, newsletters, curriculum, or other print material. You will want to use the insights you gain to develop suggestions for action at the next session. Record the findings in the journals.

Session Six

Theme: Discipleship
Texts: Joel 2:28-29
            Matthew 18:1-6
Material: Propositions 1, 7, 11, 12, 13

1. *Gathering of the community.* Introduce the session by noting the four basic purposes of the church: worship, fellowship, study, and mission. Discipleship is the living out of these aspects of the Christian life. Your four subgroups have come prepared with some reflections on the local church's ministry in relationship to the gifts of Starchildren.

2. *Group experience.* You might have the four groups of interest gather and share their finding on newsprint sheets. These clues can then be shared as a total group.

After you have a good overview of the way things are, you might spend time discussing where things could go if childlike qualities were leading the people of God. The propositions listed with this session can give you a good review of these gifts. Your people will want to refer to their journal entries for this review. Matthew 18:1-6 should be read as a statement about Jesus' support for the ministry of children. Time will be a problem in this session. You might want to chose one area of the four and plan some action. If you have a board of leadership group in your church, prepare a presentation proposing some change. For instance, get an inexpensive scrapbook (Why not a child's decoration on the front?). Remove the pages, and have your folk put together a presentation that covers: (1) Starchild qualities; (2) an analysis of the current church situation; (3) some possibilities for one aspect of the future program. Use the clippings, interviews, stories, Scripture texts for this section. You will be surprised what your folk can create in thirty minutes.

OR

You might focus on worship in which the old and the young Starchildren can fully participate. Develop a plan for getting official support for doing the service included in Part III of the User's Guide.

3. *Parting.* This will be the last time that you folk will be together. Spend some time reflecting about the safety pins. You might use the baby's blanket introduced at the beginning session. How has the Starchild led this group? What new feelings or thoughts have emerged from the persons in the class?

Ask everyone to exchange safety pins with someone else. As this is done, encourage each person to offer a blessing for the life of the other person.

You might want to call another gathering of the group if you are to make a proposal to your official board. You will need more planning if you are going to conduct the whole church worship experience in Part III.

USER'S GUIDE PART II

FOR THE FAMILIES OF CHILDREN NEWLY BAPTIZED/DEDICATED

When a babe is brought for baptism or dedication, the whole congregation is given an opportunity to rehearse some of the central facts of the faith. As the congregation makes vows to care for and nurture that small person, so it is confronted again and again with the challenge of mission. It is a time to remember the previous occasions in which those same promises have been made. It is a time to ponder just how the congregation is living out that commitment. Yet in the same service we are powerfully reminded of grace. As we rejoice that the babe already has acceptance with God as gift, we are reminded that that same gift is offered again and again to us.

In a baptism of dedication there is another level of meaning that is not always recognized. There is another challenge for the church that is seldom picked up. This challenge is not just how we shall minister to this child, but how we shall make it possible for this tiny member of Christ's body to minister to us. For instance, the person and presence of that babe is a powerful symbol of hope. Given the opportunity, the babe will touch lives with joy and tenderness.

The child can bring together in love different generations and different points of view. But all this can happen only if the parents, the congregation, and the minister or priest recognize the child's gifts. The ministry from the babe to the rest of the body is almost totally dependent upon the adults' wanting to accept it. Babies are not able to force their love on others. But parents who are willing to show their babies (and not hide them away in nurseries), to share their babies, and to encourage others to smile at and kiss the babies will find that their tiny children can have a revitalizing contribution to offer the family of Christ.

The responsibilities of parenthood are many and various. We hope that we have not underrated them. What we have tried to say is that as we have much to give to our children, so they have much to give to us. And, what is more impressive, many of their gifts to us are of a spiritual nature. Babies and small children can help their parents. From the beginning they are very much in touch with God. They carry messages of his love and acceptance. Their need to pass on these messages is as great as ours to receive them.

The authors suggest that this book and its study material be used with new parents. It may well play a part in adult nurturance that must surround infant baptism or child dedication.

Parents could be given a copy of the book. You might have folk trained to lead groups of parents with babies through the basic course of this text. The course could be offered at different times during the year.

The challenge of being enablers for Starchildren has been developed quite consistently throughout this book. However, we are ultimately supported, forgiven, and enabled to be a faithful parent by the grace of God. Many parents struggle through their important calling without the full appreciation of this gift. It does not help to judge adults for any real or imagined failures. They must be supported and enabled.

Moments of baptism/child dedication in worship provide a natural time to celebrate important spiritual truths. The adult needs to affirm that all things are possible through the grace of God as it is unfolded and experienced in the context of community.

Most of the frontline ministries of the church are really dependent on educational and spiritual support. For instance, we develop programs for youths. Yet we can never have our youths under our care for more than two or three hours a week. Therefore, we must also provide a ministry that helps parents do a better job. They are the ones who are with youths the longest time. So it is with children. Our first line of care must be strong, but the enabling of the parents themselves may be even more important.

We hope that *The Ministry of the Child* will spark many communities to study and care for young parents.

USER'S GUIDE PART III

AN ALL-AGE CELEBRATION

The authors know nothing more exciting than events where participants contribute out of their own creativity to design a culminating act of celebrative worship. It is the authors' belief that those who are moved by the Starchild within and around them will from time to time want to celebrate this and find ways of sharing it through some public witness. A celebration to which all ages are invited and in which all ages participate could provide an ideal form for such a gathering.

Such a celebration could come in a variety of formats, some of which would fit happily into the time frame and service order of regular Sunday worship. Other types of celebration will require extended time and their own special space.

Below we set out the outline of a worship event of the special-occasion type. This framework has been a vehicle for thrilling and moving family celebrations. We encourage you to use and/or modify it in any way you please. Alternate individual features of the celebration could be utilized in settings quite different from those outlined here.

This framework has worked well with all age groups in numbers of one hundred to four hundred. With appropriate adjustments it would no doubt serve smaller and larger groups. In planning a celebration such as this, take care to ensure that single adults, one-parent families, and the childless marrieds are helped to understand that this function is also for them. Celebrations that include only nuclear families will lack the extra dynamic that these folk bring. Such highly focused gatherings are not a good symbol for the all-inclusive family of God.

Both adults and children must be included in the planning and execution of this event. This is not true of every all-age service, but it is essential for this one.

Babies and toddlers will probably choose to have no overt role in the creative process. They can and must be included in the other parts of the preparation and the celebration itself. During the planning they will probably be quite happy to play on the edge of the groups. However, children older than toddlers will, if invited, make valuable contributions both in the planning and the presentation of the celebration.

A Plan for a Grand All-Age Celebration

Time Needed: Approximately two hours. A Sunday afternoon, early evening, or morning on a camp program.

Space Needed: Open space adequate to accomodate your entire group with enough room to spare for some drama or dance segments.

Leadership: *Two facilitating leaders* who are familiar with the flow and process of the event. Their job will be to lead the briefing session, organize subgroups, help subgroups with their tasks, and give such leadership as necessary (as little as possible) during the celebration.

Subgroup leaders, one for every group. These can either be chosen by the facilitating leaders and informed of their nomination at the time of group formation or the groups themselves can nominate their leaders. Both systems work quite well, but the pre-choosing of at least some leaders (e.g., music, drama, and dance) may help these groups.

Materials: Colored paper, paint, markers, masking tape, several large electrical appliance boxes, polystyrene odds and ends.

Weaving: Two-foot to four-foot strips of colored material (paper, plastic, bark, rope, or anything flexible) for weaving. There must be enough for everyone to use for weaving.

Audio-visual: Write-on slides, projector, screen (unless there is some other suitable projection surface), pens for writing on the slides, audio cassette machine with microphone.

Love feast: The two general principles here are: (1) Less is better. However, there should be enough of the goodies to ensure that everyone has at least one mouthful. (2) The foods chosen should look good, thus contrasting shapes, colors, textures, flavors. Avoid food that could be dangerous to small children (nuts, etc.). Suitable food might include apples, oranges, marshmallows, chocolate, cookies, etc.

The People and the Preparation

Seat the groups in ordered rows. Let them think, without saying anything, that this is going to be another one of those church gatherings. Divide the group into all-age subgroups, and give them a community-building exercise. Enabling leaders should try to excite groups about the celebration they will create. Announce the service theme, "Jesus Makes Us Family."

Allocate the preparation-for-worship tasks. Normally this will work out at one task per group, but other formulas could be used. The planning and preparation time is forty minutes.

The following list of tasks is by no means a definitive one, but it will serve as a useful basis for the order of service suggested.

Music. The choir group has these two guidelines: (1) All music is to be sung unaccompanied and from memory. (2) As often as possible the music chosen should be familiar to children. The choir's assignments are: (a) Prepare to lead the whole group in the singing of three hymns or inspirational songs. (b) Provide background music during times of activity in the celebration. This can be either sung or hummed.

Drama. This group will present the chosen Bible reading(s) of the day in some dramatic form. For example, they may decide to act a parable or mime three stories of Jesus with children. This group must try and include all its number in the presentation.

Prayer. There are three sections here: (1) praise, (2) confession, and (3) intercession. These sections can be given to three different units within one subgroup, or if there are many groups, they can be given to three different groups. The prayers should arise out of the life experiences and concerns of the group members. Each unit or group must then organize the appropriate content and decide how they can most meaningfully and effectively lead this prayer. The total time for each prayer must be no longer than three minutes, though it can be as short as they wish. Should groups choose, the first minute of the prayer can be used to set the mood of the prayer with some statement: acted, mimed, danced, or spoken.

Dance. The task of this group is to use movement to illustrate the essence of a short Bible passage. The text chosen should have a variety of emotional color (e.g., Isaiah, Psalms, etc.). All members of the group should participate in the presentation. After their offering this group could lead the whole celebration in some simple movements to a few key verses in the passage.

Symbols. As with the task above this could be assigned to units within one group or shared with two or three groups. Using large electrical appliance boxes as a base, this group is to design and construct several three-dimensional symbols around the theme of the service.

Weaving loom. Using a frame (probably of wood), this group is to lace string across or up and down the frame. This becomes the mesh into which the long colored pieces will later be threaded.

Food. This group is to take the party supplies and prepare them in an appetizing and artistic fashion. The emphasis is to be on breaking down the elements into small sections (e.g., peeling, slicing, breaking up, etc.).

Audio-visual. With a focus on the service theme this group will draw on the slides and record one-line statements. These slides and statements may be solely the work of this group or may come from beyond the group. Load the projector and practice putting the slides through to the accompaniment of the recorded statements.

The Celebration

Assemble the group in the worship space. Each individual is to be given a colored strip for use in the community weaving during the celebration. Seat the congregation in the round. Leave room in the center for group leadership. The order of the service should be written up on a large sheet and displayed so all can see it. It is announced that the celebration will proceed without further announcements. Groups must take their cue from the sheet. The role of the two leaders is to help the service flow. Apart from this they should do as little as possible. Prior to the service the screen and the weaving loom are placed on either side of the worship area.

Order of Service

Call to Worship .... Leader 1
Opening Song .... Choir
Prayer of Praise .... Prayer group
Word of God (read and danced) .... Dance group
Audio-Visual .... A-V group
Prayer of Confession .... Prayer group
Song .... Choir
New Testament Text .... Drama group

Offering

All move to the front to thread their colored strips in weaving frame. As this proceeds, choir provides background music.

Reflect on "Jesus Makes Us Family" with reference to the weaving just created .... Leader 2

Preparation of Love Feast .... Food group
Grace—Introduction of Meal .... Leader 1
Serving of Love Feast. Each person serves his or her neighbor. Greeting during this time.

Closing Song .... Choir

Benediction. Form one circle and all hold hands. Give opportunity for sentence prayers from those who will.

Prayer of Intercession .... Prayer group
Blessing and Dismissal .... Leader 2